Going Forth

A PRACTICAL AND SPIRITUAL APPROACH
TO DYING AND DEATH

BILL KIRKPATRICK

DARTON·LONGMAN+TODD

First published in 1997 by
Darton, Longman and Todd Ltd
1 Spencer Court
140–142 Wandsworth High Street
London SW18 4JJ

ISBN 0–232–52237–5

A catalogue record for this book is available from the British Library.

Designed by Sandie Boccacci
Phototypeset in 10/12pt Adobe Caslon by Intype London Ltd
Printed and bound in Great Britain by Page Bros, Norwich

Death is another transformation
Through which we move, an adventure,
To surpass all adventures,
An opening, an incredible moment of growth,
A graduation – Alleluia

(STEPHEN LEVINE, Who Dies?)

This book is dedicated to the memory of
Richie McMullen,
Partner and Colleague,
and so many others
who in their dying
have given me so much.
Thank you with blessings of love.

Bill

Contents

Contents

Foreword

Like any good book about death, this is at the same time a book about life. To attempt to understand the processes of dying and the experiences of bereavement involves us straight away in asking what it is to be alive; and Bill Kirkpatrick gently but insistently makes us focus on 'what turns events into experiences', what makes life an intelligible and felt unity – the soul, that much misunderstood and ignored dimension, which death inevitably points us towards. Caring for the dying, caring *about* dying, and making sense of death all require a language of the soul, not as a mysterious 'extra' in our composition but as whatever allows us room to reflect on what we are and to make contact with more than ourselves and our 'ordinary' preoccupations.

It is this aspect of the present book that will guarantee its interest and value to people other than simply pastoral carers. There is plenty of excellent practical counsel here, a variety of ways of making sense of death presented fully and with fairness. Although Bill makes no secret of his own Christian commitment, other visions are shared and set out in these pages. This is not strictly a book of theology; but it is a book seeking to evoke and to articulate wisdom, the wisdom of religious vision. To make sure that someone does not die alone is not only to offer human companionship; it is also to try and bring the dying and the bereaved into a larger conversation about life and death, which religious tradition embodies – the conversation that, for the believer, is ultimately with the maker of selves and souls, who will receive and recreate what we have been. For such a conversation, at every level, this book will be an invaluable resource.

ROWAN WILLIAMS

Introduction

This book is my response to frequent requests by colleagues and others, ordained and non-ordained, who are involved in the creation of funeral/memorial services. I offer, from my own experience, suggestions towards a practical and spiritual approach to dying and death as we move through the peak changes in our lives, especially those related to pre- and post-bereavement aspects.

Cursory reading of the literature of the world religions makes it quite clear that we should be more aware of death if we are to live our lives more fully. Death is the ultimate reality for all of us as we flow out of this time and this space into that which is beyond our comprehension. Clearly the Christian hope flows from the great Easter mystery of death and resurrection. The latter does not cancel death, rather it transfigures it.

Going Forth offers my thoughts and suggestions on how we may cope not only with the dying of another, but equally with our own daily dying. For this to occur, we need the courage of hope to become friends with what St Francis of Assisi called 'Sister Death'. 'Be praised, my Lord, through sister *bodily* death, from whom no man (woman or child) can escape'. When we accept this fact we are liberated to live our lives more fully.

I sense that the spirituality of our dying is inextricably linked with the spirituality of our living, as two sides of the same river. We become aware of this when the death of anyone who has had a profound effect on our lives leaves us grieving our loss. This highlights the fact that no one is a person totally unto his or herself.

Being alongside many dying persons of all ages (latterly with young persons dying as a result of an opportunistic infection due to AIDS), I am more aware of what I call 'a happening' as the last breath is expired. At this moment something of the uniqueness of the deceased has left the flesh and bones. I suggest that this is the leave-taking of 'the mysterious soul'. Humankind's hope for a life beyond this life is as universal today as in the ancient past. This is confirmed by the millions of near-death experiences which have been researched, verified and recorded. I liken this to a spiritual experience.

In this book I share my own bereavement experiences, aware that my response of going through a period of disconnection to reconnection is mine. This is perhaps similar, yet also different, for everyone. I know there is no single way and that the period of grief differs as one reconnects into the fullness of life again.

Our lives are guided by the 'rites of passage'. This is particularly evident during times of grief and expressed through funeral and memorial rites. In Chapter 9 an overview of the rites associated with dying and death within the major world religions offers insights into the various religions' attitudes and practices.

The funeral/memorial service is the last opportunity we have of doing something for the deceased, a time when the healing energies of bereavement may start to flow. The co-creating of such services, in the form of a 'This is Your Life' service, may help us through the initial grieving period. The Anthology section is intended to offer help in creating a funeral/memorial service.

Although I am responsible for this book, no one creates alone, therefore I am thankful to a number of people for their help: to Bishop Rowan Williams for writing the Foreword, to those who read the manuscript at differing stages, for their encouragement and forthright comments – Rev Will Baynes, Rev Jim Cotter, Sister Eva Haymann, Brian Jones, Rev Michael Paterson, Tim Robertson, Rev James Roose-Evans, Dr Heather Snidle and Rev Pat Wright – and to those who helped collate the various sections and checked information – Rev Colin Coward, James Hall, Robbie Howie, Paco Galian-Rayo, Rev Robert Mitchell, Verena Tschudin and Tony Whitehead. I am also grateful to Alan Bates, Matt Sexton, John Roddick and Candice Townson, who had between them the difficult task of deciphering my writing and finding the missing words in the script, to Jane Williams and her successor David Moloney, my editors, who encouraged me and processed the manuscript to publication, and to Pat Craddock for the cover illustration.

Looking back on the time I have been alongside the dying and the bereaved during my years as a nurse, and the past fourteen years as a minister with those living their dying through the challenges of HIV/AIDS, I have been clearly shown that all caring is circular, owing to the fact we are all wounded co-carers. Through these men and women, I have seen more clearly the liberating truth that spirituality transcends differences in religions and faiths. My hope is that this book will not only be helpful, but also a fitting tribute to them as friends who have taught me so much about daily living and daily dying. By so doing, they have encouraged me in my preparation for my own 'going forth' into the beyond.

PART ONE

1. Death, the Ultimate Mystery

Death takes us out of time, into the unknown. (KENNEDY THOM)[1]

It is important to reflect calmly again and again that death is real and comes without warning. (SOGYAL RINPOCHE)[2]

Death takes us into the unknown mystery. It is special in that it is the one aspect of reality we fear looking into. Because it involves the whole of one's self, it reminds us of our own mortality. It threatens our identities and our sense of security. It might be easier on us if we could accept that our dying begins with our conception. The only difference in our dying as individuals is the relative distances from the same reality.

Few of us would deny that death is the final triumph of nature, our inevitable physical and mental decay over our burning desire to stay young and healthy. 'Nature's final victory over the human being comes as a shock to macho, technological man; the old person who dies at eighty, written off by society, is also the husband of fifty or more years, leaving a gap in the life of his widow unknown by her forebears who expected death to end marriage within a decade; capitalism has long since stolen the communal ritual; and secularism leaves us unable to communicate with either the dead or with a God who cares for the dead.'[3]

Death, like life, is a mystery, concerning which much is still hidden from the sciences and technologies of our time. Death, no matter how painful, no matter how gentle, is a brutal event physically and even more so psychically. In death, the person we care for is taken from us even though we may do all in our power to prevent it. Death is the great divide, through which the dying person passes alone. None of us can die for another. To be there with the dying partner (I see the partner as anyone living in a committed relationship with another person), with whom we have loved and shared our lives, causes both

3

people a great deal of pain; not of the dying itself but of the lostness both are facing – something we all fear.

Most of us in the industrialised, commercialised West avoid talking about death and dying. This is usually because we are fearful of extinction. Parents want children to carry their lives forward and, even better, they visualise the arrival of grandchildren and great-grandchildren. Many fear death because they cannot imagine a life without a physical body.

In his book *The Sacred Art of Dying*, Kenneth Kramer outlines what he calls 'the three faces of death': '*physical* (the irreversible loss of brain waves, central nervous system, heart and breath functions); *psychological* (the life of quasi-consciousness, living as if having already died); and *spiritual* (the death or transformation of old patterns, habits, roles, identities and the birth of a new person)'.

Psychological death occurs when the anxiety of facing death threatens our personal identity and creativity. One of the most traumatic and shocking examples of psychological death has been experienced and explored in depth by Victor Frankl. Writing of his concentration camp experiences, he relates how 'prisoners, shortly after entering the camps, passed from their initial reaction of shock and outrage to a second response of apathy in which they achieved "a kind of emotional death" where feelings were blunted and it was easy to cease caring about being alive . . .'. Frankl suggests stopping caring in order to survive.[5] Psychological death appears as an emotional deadening which occurs when normal psychic and volitional responses are repressed. This, I suggest, has occurred more frequently since the nuclear bombing of Hiroshima. Humankind today is still living under the nuclear shadow and the threat of germ and chemical warfare. This type of death may also occur when, for whatever reasons, our creative potential is frustrated by advances (if that's what they are) in technology.

> Spiritual death is a process whereby one experiences salvation (Western) or self-awakening (Eastern) and by which the fear of death is de-repressed . . . spiritual death refers to dying while still alive, what Hindus call *moksha*, what Buddhists call *nirvana*, what Taoists call *wu wei*, what Zen calls *satori*, what Jews call living the Torah, what Christians call *rebirth* and what Muslims call *fana*. In each instance spiritual death is a rebirth in which fear of physical dying is overcome, in which internalized anxieties and doubts are de-repressed, in which a deathless spirit is realised.[6]

Our fear of dying is matched by our fear of living, nurtured through our fear of being vulnerable, of failure, of being rejected; our fear of physical, mental and social disabilities. Unless we begin to talk about death, and learn to be comfortable with our own dying we shall never be able to help others do the same. The fear of death in the West is a fundamental anxiety. This is because we all have a fear of the unknown. The fear of death has been divided into three categories by Lisl Goodman:

> Fear of death is expressed in many forms. When people are asked what it is that they fear about death, the most frequent responses fall into three categories: religiously conditioned fears, separation-abandonment fears, and existential fears. Another fear frequently expressed is of dying painfully. The fear of the process of dying is not identical with the fear of death. . . .[7]

M. Scott Peck has also written about the fear of death:

> Death is not a taker away but rather a giver of meaning . . . death is a magnificent lover . . . Like any great love, death is full of mystery and that's where much of the excitement comes from. Because as you struggle with the mystery of your death, you will discover the meaning of your life.
>
> I don't think people are afraid of death itself. What they are afraid of is the incompleteness of their life.[8]

Clearly this last statement is particularly relevant for those who die young.

Part of our coming to terms with life is accepting without fear the presence and the mystery of death in our lives, and its importance. This means recognising and accepting the fact in its stark reality – its stark nakedness – that everyone will die and that there are no exceptions. It also means recognising that the process cannot be beautified or glossed over, no matter how much we may try. It is death that can show us what is really important in our lives: awareness of death has the ability to improve the depth and quality of our lives.

It is difficult for either the dying person or those close to them not to be fearful of death and so fail to see it as 'the key' and 'the way' into that which is full of potential. If we accept the statement by Elizabeth Kübler-Ross that 'Death is the final stage of growth', then, I believe, we should think of both life and death as ongoing stages of growth. Our concern should be to live through our daily dyings into our fullest potential in this dimension of being. For me, being spiritually alive is daring to be the truth of who I am becoming as a person. In so doing I am becoming less and less fearful of my death, believing that it is a stage in my growth. This enables me to accept the death of others, although not without pain, in the awareness that in death is to be found a life that is eternal. I sense this to be true, but of course will not know until I have gone through my own dying.

As I grow into the mystery of my death, whether imminent or not, I know I am here not only to love and to be loved, but also to learn. Ideally, every happening in my life should be a creative learning experience. Nothing has helped me to learn more about the vulnerability of life and myself than the many deaths of others that I have experienced. This seems to confirm for me that daily and hourly I am being born anew, helped by an awareness of the fact that I am, daily, hourly, dying anew. The spirituality of death is the daily call to new life.

While I hope I shall be loved into 'the beyond' of this life, I know that my spiritual journey through this life and on into the next must be done within the solitude of myself. This is the one struggle no one else can undergo for me, nor I for another. What others can do for me, if they feel so inclined, is to wish me well, and let me go so that I might flow into the beyond when I am ready. Such a letting go by others dignifies not only my life but, equally important, my death.

As I attempt to understand my living and my dying, I realise that daily I am being prepared for my final death. This understanding comes through my recognising many little deaths that have and are taking place in my journeying into 'the beyond' of this life.

To be born into this dimension of being I had to 'die' first to my mother's womb. Then I had to 'die' to my mother's breast and to my mother doing everything for me as a vulnerable baby, to the security of home when I first attended school, and to junior school and my friends there when going on to high school. I have had 'to die' following each new change and each new move in order to live fully into these new places, the new spaces. Again, I had 'to die' to some of my Canadian background to live in central London. I have had 'to die' through the loss of many friends.

Death as the nourisher of life is confirmed for me through many personal losses: two sets of parents (biological and adoptive), two brothers, a great-grand nephew, a partner, many friends and colleagues (many of whom were quite young) and those who have moved to other parts of the world. I have an inner sense of the fact that when I die I will let go all that hinders my continuing growth into the mystery of the 'beyond' of this life where I shall be liberated to stand before God within the mystery of all creation.

The early Celtic Christians were aware of the fact that resurrection life is the doorway to life eternal, so much so that they claimed the day of one's death as being one's birthday. For them the way to eternal life was signposted by the various deaths in their lives. Through Jesus' dying into his resurrection, his fullness of life, we are given assurance of God's infinite presence in our daily dying into that place, that space where 'death has no more dominion over us', since 'in death shall all be made alive'.

This is not only a reminder that, in death, we are taken into the presence of the Father and Mother of us all, but also an encouragement that we shall continue developing that relationship, along with many others, more freely in that space which is beyond the comprehension of mortal life. There, we shall bring to God the truth of who we really are, without regrets or excuses. In my death, as in all deaths, my physical body will disintegrate, thereby providing space, nourishment and opportunity for those who follow on. This is part of the mystery, the spirituality, that is so unique to each one of us as we flow on from glory to glory. Clearly, death is the ultimate challenge, liberating us to flow into what so many have labelled 'the mystery'. In his book *Reaching*, Morton Kelsey writes: 'Death is birth into a new dimension of reality. For those who wish the transformation and fulfilment of heaven, death can be an entrance into greater joy than we can imagine.'[9]

For me, to answer 'What is death?' is to ask 'What is life?' It seems to me that the two questions answer each other. This echoes the Buddhist approach: 'Death is a mirror in which the entire meaning of life is reflected'. Kahlil Gibran writes, 'The beginning of life is not in matter and its end is not in the tomb. For the years that pass by are only a moment in eternal life, while the world and matter and everything that encompasses it is only a dream in the sight of that awakening which you mistakenly call the terror of death.'[10]

For me, the death of each person signifies that his or her work of co-creative loving is finished. As Edith Sitwell wrote, 'Love is not changed by death and nothing is lost and all in the end is harvest'. Another writer, T. S. Eliot, said, 'In my end is my beginning', a reminder that life is full of endings and beginnings. It seems to me that the completeness of life is the death of life as we know it. It is the total release of the person into the life of love's mystery unending

7

– a fact that becomes a reality as we learn to look at the life that so enriched us instead of the death and the departing, and we try to accept and recognise that in love there is no departing. Death in life leads to life in death.

Clearly, what we think about death puts life into question. In asking the eternal question of life, we discover God at its centre, joining life and death together for all time, in time and out of time. As St Paul reminds us, 'As in Adam all die, even so in Christ shall all be made alive'.

2. Flowing into the Beyond

Living in the face of dying. (SIMON BAILEY)[1]

Death is the point where we finally come face to face with ourselves. (SOGYAL RINPOCHE)[2]

Dying is as natural as being born and is a continuing process between our first breath and our last. It is a reminder of our biological nature. It is also a reminder that we are part of the natural world of earthquakes, floods and storms, of fire and wind, of disease and infirmity, of the cycle of life and death, death and life.

Death shatters our security. It forces significant changes in the economic and social status of the bereaved. Death is accompanied by absence, by loneliness and by longing. It can also bring into being a period of disorganisation for significant others – partner, family, friends (particularly so for the partner and immediate family).

Much of my work, especially during the past fourteen years, has been alongside people who are dying. I have come to recognise that they, like myself, will die in the uniqueness of their aloneness. No one can die for another, just as no one can be born for another. Our birth and our dying proclaim this, even though we may be supported in our dying. If we are to be involved in this ministry alongside the dying, we must be aware of our own mortality. If we look closely, we shall realise that we have died many times during our lives. Every major change is a form of dying. We are born to die that we might live our fullest potential into the mystery labelled life.

It is important to remember the following points in our attempts to be alongside those who are dying:

- We need to be emotionally and psychologically comfortable with dying and with those who are in the process of becoming bereaved.
- We can risk being acceptable only when the other person senses that we have confronted our own fears about dying.

- We must recognise that to deny any emotional connection with the dying person is to increase the psychological pain of his or her illness.

If I am to be realistically alongside the person who is dying I must first ask myself the following questions (although not when I am tired, depressed or going through the pain of recent bereavement):

1. Who would *I* like to be at *my* side, to embrace *me* as *I'm* dying?
2. Who do *I* think would really miss *me*?
3. What impression would *I* leave behind?
4. What single word would give meaning to *my* life?
5. What have *I* to put right before *I* die?
6. What relationship have *I* to put right before *I* die?
7. Who have *I* to say thanks to before *I* die?
8. From whom should *I* seek forgiveness?
9. To whom should *I* offer forgiveness?
10. What should *I* like to achieve before *I* die?
11. What kind of service would *I* like?
12. Whom would *I* specifically invite?
13. Whom would *I* not invite and why?

Daily I am being made aware of how valuable the gift of listening is, not only for the person dying, but also for the person attempting to offer care that is meaningful and with a confidence that comes through being authenticated and affirmed by love and nurtured by the hope that enriches the dying.

As a minister, I must have the time and patience to encourage the person to speak openly about his or her dying if that is their wish. Equally, I have no right to force the person to talk about it if it would be unacceptable to them. Yet I am aware of the fact that most people know whether or not they are dying and many unwillingly collude with others in the pretence that they are 'not dying'.

My basic ministry with both the dying and the bereaved is to listen – to listen attentively and with such care that they can listen comfortably to themselves with a confidence that comes from being valued. Listening enables me to decide whether or not I should open the discussion about their dying. If I do decide to, I might use the following questions:

1. Would you like to tell me about your illness?
2. How ill do you believe you are?

3. What have the doctors/nurses/other care team members/your family said about your illness?
4. What ideas or thoughts have you about what they have said with regard to your illness?
5. What do you feel or believe about illness?
6. What do your partner/wife/husband/parents or other members of your family believe?
7. What do you believe they know?

Essential in all pastoral care, especially in the care of the dying, is the ability to listen with the whole of oneself. This means that I will have come to this person with no hidden agenda, with no responsibility for whether the person lives or dies – that is out of my hands – and in the realisation that to care means being detached enough to be able to cope with caring, and that is extremely difficult. I am there to listen to the dying person's attempts to express whatever he or she wishes to express. People express themselves in different ways but there are often common areas of concern:

- fear of loneliness, hopelessness, uncertainty, powerlessness, the unknown, insecurity, non-existence, rejection;
- fear of losing physical strength, energy, weight, body image, appearance, independence, physical and mental control, eyesight;
- fear of losing partner, family, friends, social environment, home, work – ultimately, life itself.

Whatever the cause of the person's dying he or she will probably express in some form or other the following desires:

- to be as free from pain as possible;
- to be allowed to die with dignity;
- to be embraced by the most significant person(s) in his or her life;
- to find some meaning – an answer to 'What happens to me when I die?';
- to know that they are acceptable and loved by God;
- to have a real say in where the dying should take place, whether home, hospice or hospital;
- to know that some form of pastoral care is available, e.g. prayer, the sacraments or the gift of silence;
- to know that being the recipient of pastoral care does not require prior confession and penitence;

- for those whose lifestyles are not generally understood, to know whether they will be condemned to hell.

There are other pastoral duties too for those caring for the dying:

- promoting self-acceptance and helping the dying person to come to terms with their own personal identity;
- encouraging the healing of rifts between family and/or friends;
- suggesting the making of a will if at all possible;
- suggesting the planning of the funeral or memorial.

Caring for the dying person includes caring too for the partner, the family and friends. This also means encouraging them to:

- accept the person behind the illness;
- accept the medical/nursing/social/spiritual care in accordance with the person's wishes;
- accept the person's wish on whether or not to continue with aggressive treatment or to let nature take its course;
- accept the funeral service arrangements made by the deceased or the person(s) closest to him or her;
- remember that the young person's service is for celebrating his or her life – more often than not it will not be traditional;
- accept the fact, however painful, of the dying person's goodbye;
- accept the fact that many wish to die in silence, often alone, knowing they are surrounded by love – or perhaps with only the most important person in his or her life present;
- accept that the time of death is that person's 'now' for flowing into the beyond. It is important not to hold the person from going in his or her own time.

We need to be aware of the fact that a great many people, as they die, wish to have control of their dying for as long as possible. For some this may be up to within an hour of their last breath. This enables the person to die with dignity and is a call for us to respect unreservedly this most sacred moment for the person who is dying their own unique death. It is a dying that is different from all others because each comes to this peak moment in his or her life with their own life history and experience. There is no 'normal' way of dying that is common to everyone.

A Charter of Rights for the Dying Person

1. To be treated as a unique human being.
2. To be treated as an equal.
3. To be treated as an adult, not as a child.
4. To participate in all decisions concerning their care.
5. To be cared for by those qualified to do so.
6. To be involved in their own care.
7. To have all questions answered directly and truthfully.
8. To have the right to express emotions.
9. To expect the carer to be a non-judgemental listener.
10. To be encouraged through the upholding of hope.
11. To discuss, or not discuss, as they wish, religion, and spiritual or other experiences of dying.
12. To die in the place of their own choosing.
13. To have the body respected in accordance with their own wishes.
14. To be treated with the dignity of love and hope.

Those of us involved in this area of care need to encourage the co-creative potential of every death into the mystery of love. I believe that the death of each person signifies that the work of love is finished for him or her, irrespective of the length of that person's life. Some of the most beautiful pieces of music have been left unfinished, cut short by the death of the composer. Often it is death that reveals what is important in our lives.

There are two meanings we can give to death. Either it can mean the end of our identity, or it can be a doorway or an opening to eternal life. In many cases, death is not as great a problem for the person dying as for those who are in the process of being bereaved. The final and most fundamental task for the dying person and their family is to re-establish those connections that will give their final separation meaning. This is a stage where those involved hover between complete acceptance and denial of the imminence of death. It is stage in which conversations about death and loss may alternate with conversations about the ongoing life of the partner, family or circle of friends.

Few who are ill with an opportunistic infection such as AIDS, die suddenly. Therefore there is often time to prepare and to make peace, to embrace the dying person with love. Sudden and unexpected death (e.g. suicide or sudden heart attack) are rare and it is a fact that a sudden death often elicits more grief than one is prepared for, though in a sense one is never fully prepared. Being alongside the grieving person is never easy: I have often felt helpless, not knowing what to say or do. This is particularly evident after a sudden death, whether a result of accident or suicide. But caring may simply mean being there in the silence, where pain can speak to pain in a way that words never could, being attentive to the person's needs and realising there are no answers. For some, grieving is difficult if they have not yet fully grieved for a previous death or loss (for example, the mother who said, 'How can I grieve for my son, when I never grieved for my stillborn baby who died twenty-five years ago?').

In grief, many people turn to sex to seek comfort or reduce the tension of extreme physical, mental or social pain. It becomes a mode of survival, of affirmation. The loss of a partner is also, in many instances, accompanied by a deep sense of sexual deprivation. This may occur the first time one sleeps alone, and may stimulate the desire for comfort by initiating a sexual act with some friend, a casual acquaintance or even a stranger. This need may also occur for hormonal and/or psychological reasons that often overrule our reason or will.

Some of the determining factors in the different ways of grieving are:

- The mode of death – whether it is natural or self-induced.
- The involvement of the partner and other family members in the person's dying.
- The age of the person who has died, considered against their life-expectancy.
- The existence of multiple stresses between family members and the deceased.
- The social and economic changes resulting from the death.
- The support available from social and other networks.
- The nature of the relationship – whether secure or ambivalent, dependent or co-dependent.

The process of grieving affects people in as many different ways as there are differing types of personalities. A bereaved person can become fixated on what has been lost, fearing that they will never be able to rediscover those attributes so valued in their deceased partner. Grieving is made easier for a bereaved partner when both families recognise the partnership and are able, through their own bereavement, to support the surviving partner. But this does not always happen. For instance, the family of the deceased partner may try to prevent the survivor attending the funeral service and, if they are able to obtain access to the home, they may even attempt to claim everything and destroy any sign of the relationship. Such action has led to the suicide of the surviving partner in some cases.

As the grieving lessens, remembering gradually becomes a celebration of the cherished aspects of the relationship. The bereaved person begins, little by little, to believe that he can learn from his warm memories of the relationship and he may discover within himself the projected attributes of his partner. Self-acceptance allows the development of a post-bereavement identity and the shaping of a new life, often taking on the roles played by the deceased person.

To aid the bereavement process there needs to be an opportunity to take part in rites of passage that will enable us to grow through our grieving. The Christian Church provides such rites for its members, as do other religious faiths. However, there is also an innate need for such rites by those who are outside the faith of their families or their community.

Spiritual care of the bereaved often includes very simple things – perhaps just offering a cup of tea. The most important way we can help may be through the gifts of touch and hearing, being able to sit there without saying or doing anything and not feel guilty or embarrassed. The art of listening is important. By paying full attention we can encourage the bereaved person to move from immobility, perhaps a result of fear, to action nurtured by hope.

This also applies to people's fears about themselves. When Mary came to see me she immediately lay on the floor, with arms crossed as though in a coffin. In her own time she informed me that she had just had the result of an HIV test which proved positive. When Mary was informed of her HIV status all she could hear was 'HIV/AIDS = Death'. Although she received both pre- and post-test counselling, Mary could not hear that HIV/AIDS equals challenge. I encouraged her to see her health adviser and to make contact with others recently informed as being positive. With her permission I contacted her health adviser, who saw her every day for several weeks. I also saw her occasionally. Now, five years later, she is spending time being alongside others who have just been diagnosed. Mary is a clear example of moving through immobility towards the mobility of concern for others.

This attentive presence says to the other person:

- You are full of value.
- You are deserving of respect.
- You are being given space to sort out your thoughts, your concerns, your relationships and your hopes.
- You are letting me fulfil my commitment to you.

In addition, many a dying person receives much comfort through touch. Touch tells them that they are still of value whatever their physical or mental condition. So often touch speaks louder than words. It restores a sense of value. It conveys unquestioning acceptance. It facilitates a release of emotional feelings. It communicates where words fail. It expresses concern and compassion. We should never under-estimate the fact that touch is the simplest and most healing form of human contact. But we have to be careful how we use it and ask permission first. If someone has been physically or sexually abused, touch may awaken painful feelings, making it difficult for the person to accept touch positively. Also, in some cultures it can be very offen-sive to make physical contact.

Alongside the ministry of presence there is also the ministry of absence. The dying tire easily. We all need to be sensitive to the needs of the person we are visiting and mindful of how long to stay and when to slip away. Some may feel guilty about sending for the pastor or other caring persons. We can minimise this by saying, 'If ever I arrive and you do not feel like seeing me, please send me away. I will not be offended, only pleased I can do something for you at that moment.'

There is no doubt in my mind that as carers we are not alongside the dying person to lay down the law, to preach, to condemn, or to proselytise. That would be religious blackmail and certainly not an act of love nurtured by hope. I was told of the experience of a young man who asked to see a priest. When the priest arrived he stood at the end of the bed to avoid any physical contact and said, 'the pain you are suffering should reduce the pain you will suffer after death'. He got no further, as the young man yelled at him to get out! His mother stopped going to church because she felt it was no longer possible to identify her image of Christ with such a judgemental response from a priest. It is crucial that we as pastors remember the person's need to be loved for his or her own sake and clearly with no other motives. We are there to demonstrate the unconditional acceptance of God, who I believe does not know how to reject, and the forgiveness of God is a constant gift to us, no matter what our past wrongs or shortcomings. The best promise made by God is still to come, in that our dying is 'the gateway to fullness of life'.

Being alongside the dying is to be consciously aware of one's own dying, to recognise we are all vulnerable to death at any time. To be there with the dying person is to be involved in one of life's most sacred activities, the leave-taking of that person as they commit themselves into the beyond in their own time. I have seen changes occur in people who are dying once they have grasped and accepted the fact that they are in the final stages of growth. I have seen how dying has released those factors that inform us that life is for living and dying – such factors as compassion, courage, acceptance, patience, faith, hope and love. They encourage us to look within and build upon the stillness of peace within our inner selves. It is from within this stillness that we reach out to one another. Spiritual care has more to do with *being* than with *doing*, as together we wait on God. Elizabeth Kubler-Ross reminds us:

> Death is the final stage of growth in this life. There is no total death. Only the body dies. The self or spirit or whatever you may wish to label it, is eternal. You may interpret this in any way that makes you comfortable.[3]

Actively assisting people to die is not new. It has gone on throughout the history of humankind. I suspect that some may have acceded to their dying partner's wish to be released from this life. They are usually partners who love each other very much. I respect their maturity and integrity, when on the whole society's attitude is against any form of assisted death.

The ministry of the pastor, the carer, to the dying person is to be a *presence of hope* in any way that will enable the dying person to die with dignity and confidence in God, the ultimate Father/Mother of all creation, so at the last the person may be able to say, 'Into your hands, your heart, O Lord, I commend my all, knowing I am acceptable just as I am, with my weaknesses and strengths'. To be accepting of one's self, 'warts and all', is to be released. It is also an acceptance of each other's uniqueness. To the extent that we are able to do this we are enriching and extending our living fully into our dying.

For the Christian-orientated person another way of understanding this death/rebirth process is through the three integral elements of '*confession* (a death to the fear of making public one's psychologically deadening anxieties); *conversion* (a death to one's prior ego-controlled tendencies and a birth to new self-awareness); *confirmation* (a death to the monologue of mistrust and the birth of compassion)'.[4]

Making known to others (or one other person) our psychological anxieties about death can be an act of compassion towards oneself. This new birth begins through the act of confession, if you like, through the telling of the story – a story that needs to be understood and valued for its uniqueness, either formally, as in a sacramental sense, or informally, as between two soul friends. This confession, no matter what form it takes, usually expresses a sense of having missed the mark of perfection, a sense of incompleteness, an awareness of character flaws and missed opportunities. It is the divided self attempting to become undivided, more fully one's real self. The person may feel divided from him or herself, from others and from God. More often than not this is nurtured by a constant attitude of guilty self-reproach.

Conversion through confession, however offered, opens the way towards rebirth, liberation into a fullness of life. As William James writes:

> To be converted, to be regenerated, to receive grace, to experience religion, to gain an assurance, are so many phrases which denote the process, gradual or sudden, by which a self hitherto divided, and consciously wrong, inferior and unhappy, becomes unified and consciously right, superior and happy, in consequence of its former hold upon religious realities.[5]

This process is not available only to Christians affiliated to specific institutional churches – it is the extension of God's unconditional love, as mirrored in the life and ministry of Jesus the Christ. To say that a person is converted means 'that religious ideas, previously peripheral in consciousness, now take a central place, that religious aims form the habitual center of energy'.[6]

Conversion is the result of our daily spiritual growth. This comes about through co-creative dialogue nurtured by the three dimensions – acceptance, affirmation and confirmation:

> Buber distinguished and recognised the relation between three dimensions of dialogue – acceptance, affirmation and confirmation. The three move from a generic acceptance (e.g. I accept you as a person like myself), to a specific affirmation of one's unique personhood (e.g. I affirm you in your difference from myself), and to

a confirmation of the other (e.g. I trustingly validate you both now and in the future).[7]

Through causing the other person to feel fully present and in knowing that one's own self is made present by the other, there exists together the mutuality of affirmation, of acceptance and of confirmation, enabling us to experience our dying in an anticipatory way. It seems that most sacred traditions have ways of encouraging us to bring death consciously back into our daily lives and thus to anticipate our dying.

> To die spiritually is to experience a dying from which one is rebirthed, resurrected in a new holistic way of being more fully alive. Instead of termination of human creativity, our study of the presence of death in life restored the original interpretation of life and death, of dying before dying.[8]

What can I say? What can I do? The most helpful and most basic of acts is that of listening in such a way that we hear what the other person is saying, whether verbally or non-verbally. It is crucial that we listen carefully to the dying or the grieving person's feelings. And it is of equal importance to listen deeply to our own feelings. Carefully listening includes doing whatever one can to alleviate suffering (physical, emotional, social and spiritual) through the empathy of compassion. It also involves treating the dying person as a living being, respecting the person's wishes for information that is honest and factual about his or her condition, encouraging the person to talk about his or her illness, dying and death, and allowing the person as much control as possible throughout the journey into the beyond.

We must accept the fact, that, more often than not, there are no right words to offer the person who is dying. We cannot and should not try to plan what we will, or will not, say ahead of time; that is a means of finding words of comfort for ourselves rather than for the person who is dying. As long as we have the integrity and desire to respond with the empathy of compassion the right words will come through silences shared.

In order to liberate ourselves into being of service it is crucial to listen to one's own denials, fears and anger towards one's own dying. To be an effective listener one must acknowledge and be prepared at times to express whatever feelings the situation may give rise to. Dr Kübler-Ross has outlined five stages in the dying person's experience – denial, anger, bargaining, depression, acceptance. To these I would add two further stages: waiting and transformation. These stages can have a profound effect on those working with or being alongside the dying person. Throughout all these stages, the one thing that persists is hope – hope for a miracle, hope for a new drug, hope for a new diagnosis, hope for a death with dignity. Hope is something the person must never be deprived of.

When we are with a dying person we need to be aware of the transformational possibilities within the experience of dying. This will be all the easier if we are aware of the possibility within ourselves. With such an awareness we will then be able to:

- be a caring presence at whatever level is possible;
- listen attentively as an equal;
- touch gently, when appropriate;
- avoid all psychological or religious jargon;
- find out where the person is hurting;
- contact the dying person's faith practitioner when requested to do so.

A sharing of our daily dying before our actual death is to experience something of the mystery of our rebirth. Through learning to die, daily death is transformed from something we are fearful of into an opportunity not only to offer, but also to receive, love. For the Christian, the cross is the ultimate symbol of life and death, and death and resurrection are hidden in the activity within the cross. Nurtured by the reality of an all-embracing love, we can experience – within and beyond our dying – our 'going forth'.

3. Spirituality of the Dying

This is a good day to die.
The sun will rise tomorrow.
This is a good day to die.
The river flows endlessly.
This is a good day to die.
I follow my bliss into the Earth.

(CRAZY HORSE)[1]

Spirituality of the dying is also a spirituality of the living. Christian spirituality is based on the gospel of love and forgiveness taught by Jesus. Others might interpret it as the way we are within ourselves and with others in different situations. The *Dictionary of Christian Spirituality* defines it as 'a word which has come into vogue to describe those attitudes, beliefs, practices, which animate people's lives and help them to reach out towards super-sensible realities'.[2] An alternative understanding is offered by John Fortunato in *AIDS: The Spiritual Dilemma.* He writes:

> . . . by *spiritual* I allude to the journey of the soul – not to religion itself but to the drive in humankind that gives rise to religion in the first place. I have in mind the software on the computer of life, not its hardware; the program as it runs, not the data to be input or the machine that processes it or even the printout. By *spiritual* I am referring to that aura around all our lives that gives what we do meaning, the human striving toward meaning, the search for a sense of belonging.[3]

In our dying we are often pushed into asking basic questions of spirituality – Who am I in my dying? What do I really want? Where am I going? What am I really fearful of? How can I die into the truth of my real self that I might be more fully alive in my dying, my flowing into the beyond?

Through being alongside many people in their dying, I have seen

21

them come alive, as though touched by some inner response to the activity of dying. This suggests to me that life is more about the *now* moments than about being in time; it is more about flowing out of time, into the mystery of the unknown; it's about living with passion in the fullness of our dying, unencumbered by life.

Many have reminded me of the importance of letting go and letting God be in all that we are involved in. In this sense many are aware that it is here in the process of dying that the utter sacredness of their lives is to be found and acknowledged. Here is the process where the psyche outgrows its human limitations, as they go forth into the cloud of unknowing, where the human spirit meets with the mysterious unknown – where humanity's mystery meets with God's mystery. I have increasingly come to an awareness that dying is the ultimate spiritual experience – a constant activity in the very centre of life. For me this is affirmed by those who have made their transition into the mystery labelled death. The different ways in which they have come to terms with their dying appears to create an awareness of another dimension as they prepare to flow into the beyond.

I remember my first encounter with death – a robin killed by a cat. I remember taking its mangled body, putting it in a box and burying it in the garden, while crying, and afterwards saying with real conviction, '*my* robin will fly again'. Our awareness of the mystery of death may help us to prepare for flowing into the beyond of our life's span, whether that span is long or short. Being caught up in this flow does not make us other-worldly; rather it is preparing the path away from the superficial in our daily lives, while at the same time releasing us into a greater awareness of how our lives are being nurtured by spirituality.

In my work with people who are dying, I have discovered that many are spiritual rather than religious. They are open to the mystery labelled God, rather than to organised religion which they see as an impersonal framework held together by the fabric of creeds and doctrines. It is because of this that we need to be acutely aware that in our society the words 'religious' and 'spiritual' are not necessarily synonymous. When we take time to listen and consider, we may find that many people feel religion to be irrelevant in their lives. They will say quite often, 'I am not religious, but I am spiritual' or 'I have my own beliefs about God'. The spiritual may be seen in the wishes expressed concerning a funeral/ memorial service – for a priest to officiate, for the 23rd Psalm, the

Lord's Prayer or the St Francis prayer to be included, or selections from Fauré's Requiem, for example.

The spiritual may also be encountered in such questions as: Is there a God? If so, where? Why does God allow suffering? Is there a heaven? Where is hell? Will God accept me? These questions suggest that spirituality is nurtured by a search for meaning. It evokes the use of 'mystery' language rather than 'God' language. It is also a search for an identity that will survive death, through a recognition and acceptance that we are related to the whole of creation, visible and invisible. People need to have their hopes affirmed as each in his or her own way maintains a dignity through the fulfilment of their basic spiritual needs.

Any mention of spirituality must take into consideration New Age spirituality. Today there is a fundamental paradigm shift occurring between the established way and new ways of expressing one's spirituality, especially by the young. It is important that those ministering with and to the dying take this into account, as part of being fully attentive to the dying and the bereaved person. Writing about New Age spirituality in *The Art of Dying*, Patricia Weenolsen says:

> I suspect that (1) the new sense of immediacy in the spiritual relationship, (2) the long-denied recognition and acceptance of unusual experiences and alternate realities, (3) the resumption by women of their rightful place in spiritual guidance (a move that the traditional religions have resisted), (4) the honouring and union of diversity in peoples and religions, (5) the oneness with nature and resulting practical earth stewardship necessary for human survival, (6) the accessibility of the transcendent, the mystical and the rapturous, (7) the alternative healing that is not necessarily cure, and (8) the infusion into daily life of spiritual meaning and mindfulness will survive. Perhaps they will be incorporated into traditional religions where the mystical has flourished. They will survive because, once found, they are too precious to sacrifice to an institution that, in some respects, suffers from hardening of the arteries. Reciprocally, the New Age itself must guard against institutionalisation and must remain fluid and permeable enough to grow.[4]

True spirituality leads us by various pathways into the unknown, into the holy, mysterious processes of living and dying, away from certainty and towards a larger all-inclusive questioning. It awakens us to our own unique and sacred self-identity and an understanding that we are not persons having a spiritual being, but rather spiritual beings having a human experience. Being involved in the spirituality of life should lead us quite naturally to being involved in the spirituality of dying.

Two basic questions that the priest or pastor must ask him or herself on first contact with the dying or bereaved person are: (1) How can I recognise and accept where this person is coming from spiritually? (2) How best can I meet these needs? This can be easily answered if the person identifies with a faith community where there is a body of accumulative knowledge and experience to draw on. But meetings with such people today are becoming increasingly rare. So, how are we to be alongside those who have experienced their particular faith tradition to be unhelpful, condemning or severely judgemental, or who may never have had a real connection with religion, as is so often the case? What might spiritual care mean for this particular dying or bereaved person? Stoll suggests that we can start by asking ourselves: What is the person's concept of God or duty?[5] What is the person's source of hope or strength? What is the significance of religious practice or rituals to this person? What is the person's perceived relationship between spiritual beliefs and his/her state of health? The aim here is to identify areas of spiritual need and to plan appropriate support.[6]

Spiritual care ensures that the dying person's needs are met, through constant reassurance, understanding, empathy, unassuming friendship (soul-friending) and access to the sacraments and rituals, thereby giving them a sense of being acceptable, affirmed through the loving that nurtures the hope for this person at all times. It is through sharing the spirituality of life that the dying person can explore freely his or her doubts, fears, beliefs or non-beliefs without ridicule or rejection. The listening ear of the soul-friend opens the way for the spiritual ministry of 'just being there' for the dying person. This can be the best kind of human bridge between this life and the next. Caring for someone who is dying is demanding spiritual work. It calls for courage to face the various challenges when confronting death, requiring us to accept limits in life and to let go of the will to control.

Spiritual care includes being concerned about physical and mental pain which are often the source of spiritual pain. Being concerned, we will know that pain is a subjective rather than an objective experience. Thankfully pain is being increasingly recognised as an ailment with negative consequences. Today there is a growing recognition that pain is unhealthy, stressful and anxiety-provoking and can interfere with normal body–mind functioning. I believe it is our responsibility to encourage the dying person to speak honestly about his or her pain, in the awareness that the easing of pain is a mutual service. We need to encourage the person to express their needs for pain relief, be this in physical, mental, social or spiritual ways. We must never say to the person suffering pain, 'Oh, I know how you feel'. This is an impossibility because we are not that person, we may be able to empathise through the pain we have experienced, but that is all.

It is almost impossible when someone is in pain to see how any good can come out of suffering. As ministers we must ask ourselves whether there can be any spiritual benefit from pain. In her book *The Art of Dying*, Patricia Weenolson writes:

> Not all suffering can be relieved. So a review of the possible spiritual uses of pain may be helpful to some of you, although, to be honest, I'd rather not have to go through this spiritual lesson.
>
> Pain arouses compassion in others, which, if they act upon it, may be the salvation of their souls.
>
> Pain, if it doesn't shrink our minds, makes us pause and evaluate our lives, selves, and relationships. It gives us time and justification to do so.
>
> Pain may open us to others, and them to us, bringing us closer to one another.
>
> Finally, pain snips at the threads that bind us to life – snip, snip, and we are less and less attached, bits of us floating skyward like a bouquet of balloons released one at a time, until they are far too far away from us to see them pop in the increasingly rarified atmosphere.[7]

I believe there are a number of shoulds in spiritual care of which ministers of whatever faith should be aware:

- They should be aware of the need to be an attentive listener who hears the whole person.
- They should be prepared to honour the dignity of every person, whatever his or her state physically, mentally, socially and/or spiritually, all of which impinge on each other.
- They should be able to offer the empathy of acceptance and hope.
- They should be able to understand the 'Why?' arising from the anger and pain of the person who is being bereaved of the self.
- They should be able to face objectively the ethical and moral questioning which may arise.

- They should have faced the issues of their own bereavement and dying and be welcoming of it in due course. Unless they have done so they will be unable to face multiple losses and the attendant experiences of bereavement.

Dying is the supreme challenge in life. When we are brought face to face with the processes of dying it may lead to the discovery of an unexpected courage to face in hope the inevitable.

Some may need to be assured that they are with God in their dying. Others may need to be helped to forgive and to receive forgiveness. 'Do you think God will ever forgive me for my sins, my falling short of the mark?' is a question often asked. Surely the only answer is that forgiveness is the very nature of God. The question that needs to be asked of the person is, 'Can you forgive yourself?' They can be helped to do this by remembering the good they have done and through the forgiveness of themselves and others. Thankfully all religions stress the power of forgiveness, a power never more necessary, nor more deeply felt, than when someone is dying and preparing the way for completing his or her journey into the mystery.

Sometimes in the comfort of an unobtrusive presence the person will say things of great spiritual depth, even when they insist, 'I'm not a believer, I'm not religious'. The offering of the empathy of compassion appears in some way to release an inner wisdom, enabling the person to discover his or her own truth. This self-removal of masks and the superficiality of everyday living allows the person to be more open and sensitive to the mystery and the meaning of life and his or her dying.

The dying need to know that God loves them. They should be enabled to sense through our pastoral care the empathy of God's acceptance of them. As pastors, we should try to be the heart of God reaching out to the heart and soul of the dying person. In this way they will know the experience of being embraced by the soul of God, as they themselves are being embraced by their own unique soul. We become this kind of acceptable pastor when we speak from within our own lived knowledge of dying and bereavement. This is why it is so crucial that pastors to the dying are men and women who, through prayer, will speak and simply 'be there' for the other person, offering hope as they go through 'the dark night of the soul', each in the reality of their own dying.

When alongside a person who is dying you are forced to ask yourself where this courage, this hope, this meaning and sense of dignity come from. You wonder how the mystery of another's dying enriches your own life and your ability to carry on. If we are attentive to the dying person and are humble enough to allow him or her to be alongside us, we soon recognise that all caring is circular – that the dying person and the carer may be seen to be co-carers one of the other through being totally present to each other.

Spiritual caring for another will be more realistic when the minister recognises his or her need for care. I remember attending a conference at which Dr Sheila Cassidy spoke and she offered two powerful pieces of advice for those who would be carers in the spiritual work of being with and alongside the dying, the grieving and the bereaved. I feel they are crucial to all who are offering friendship along with whatever sacraments or rituals are requested. First, she referred to the fact that the Christian carer should try always to take the paschal overview of suffering and that he or she should keep in focus the harsh reality of suffering and the mind-boggling truth of the resurrection – life after death. She also said that the requirement for survival is that we have the humility to know our limitations, to take time out. 'No one, but no one can work day in, day out with the afflicted (the dying) without respite (care). Don't be daft, God called you to look after his people, to be caring – not to burn out.'[8]

This is good, sound advice, grounded in reality. Clearly the spirituality of the dying nurtures the spirituality of the living, both based on mutual compassion.

4. The Mysterious Soul

The soul is that which makes things alive. (SHELDRAKE and FOX)[1]

I cannot see my soul, but I know 'tis there. (EMILY DICKINSON)

I no more understand the mystery of the soul than I do the mystery of God or love. For me, words like 'soul', 'God', 'Love' are coded, open-ended, incapable of being fully deciphered. I suspect that they are partly decoded as we live out our lives to the best of our abilities. The very idea of the soul underscores the importance of being me, of being a member of the community of all God's people. With this in mind, I recognise and accept that each and every relationship calls for recognition and response if the soul is to be honoured as sacred. I feel that the soul may be the sacred energy of creativity. It is, I feel, the thread linking us in the 'here and now' with the 'there and then'.

In my desire to gain some insight into the nature of the soul (in so far as this is possible), I feel I must first come to know my own soul. I do so by asking such questions as: What is my soul? What does my soul require of me? What is the relationship between myself and my soul? How does my soul impinge on all areas of my life? I am aware that alongside such centuries-old questions as 'What is my soul?' are others such as: Where did I come from? Why am I here? Where will I go when I die? Where am I coming from at this period in my life?

I am becoming aware that *I am my soul* and that it embraces the whole of me and is also the invisible fabric of my being Bill. I have a sense of 'inner knowing', tinged with some uncertainty, that my soul is impregnated with the mystery of God. It is, I suspect, a mystery nurturing another mystery that is my deepest self. I believe it was Dr Pusey who made the statement: 'What the soul is to the body, God is to the soul. The life of the body is the soul, the life of the soul is God.' This implies for me that the soul *is* life and must be nurtured by the very ordinariness of my life, through my daily acts of dying from within the gift of my daily living. I believe the soul communicates something of itself through the language of beauty, music, art, poetry, laughter, joy, nature and in the pain of suffering and vulnerability. Some of the most awesome moments of the soul's presence for me have occurred when I am being attentive to the intense silences of a dying person and I become aware that we are not alone. During such silences I ponder on whether death is the interplay between the mysteries of the inner and the outer worlds.

For many years I have asked myself whether having a soul is equal to being alive. I began to think about this during my early days as a nurse. I remember nursing a young man who had been unconscious following a serious motorcycle accident. Before he died, he briefly regained consciousness, sat up in bed and spoke for the first time since his accident. As he did this he appeared to be looking beyond me, as though he could see someone he knew. He said quite clearly, 'Helen, it's so good to see you again'. The young man then lay back. He never spoke again, and died within a few hours. I later asked his parents who Helen was. It turned out that she was his grandmother who had died the previous year in the same week. Their son adored her and used to call her 'Grandma Helen'. She was the only woman in the family history known as Helen.

I have asked myself many times why this experience had such a lasting effect on me. Was it a spiritual experience? Was it because I was part of this man's dying? Was it because he was so young? I remember feeling the presence of someone else while I was preparing him for the chapel of rest. It may have been that I had become very close to him; he was, after all, 'my patient, my responsibility'. Many times throughout my life as a nurse, and later as a priest, I have been at the bedside of a dying person and sensed that something vital was leaving the body. Was it the soul, the life energies? Once the person has died, I have felt the presence of another in the room. Was it the soul hovering around? Was it a soul from beyond taking the newly released soul into the beyond?

Being alongside those who are seriously ill or dying causes me to ask the question: Is the soul the energiser of life, the nurturer of the person's body and mind? Could one say that the soul energises life, while death liberates the soul from the confines of the body? Can we say that the soul is the vital thread that links the mind with the body, ideas with life, spirituality with the world, person with person, and the 'all' of creation?

In writing this book, I felt I had to attempt to write about the mystery labelled 'soul'. I am a novice in understanding the nature of the soul, yet I feel I have been touched by many souls, especially those who loved or still love me. It seems to me that the very idea of the soul reminds us of the importance, the vulnerability and the strengths of every person. It is the *holy ground* of each person's life.

But what is the soul? This is a question that has been constantly asked and debated by men and women throughout history. Clearly the ancient mythologies and the different world faiths have varying perspectives on what the soul is or is not. Writing from a Christian perspective, I see it as having an eternal value that the body does not have. When we talk about the resurrection of the body, are we in fact talking about the resurrection of the body of energies that we label 'soul'?

In seeking some affirmation of my own thinking about the soul, I have been reading the thoughts of many others. The following extracts from some of these authors may assist the reader in his or her pondering on the mysterious soul.

> The soul or spirit of the human individual may be characterised variously: by Hinduism as the divine self, by Buddhism as the product of conditions and causes, and by Judaism, Christianity and Islam as the core of the individual person, partaking of his or her choices and deeds. From the perspective of ontology, we note that Buddhism does not conceive of the soul as ultimately real; it parts company with the Hindu and Jain concept of the soul as identified with the divine self (*Atman*). The Abrahamic religions understand the personal soul to be real, yet at the same time, distinct from God, who is fundamentally other and distinct from his creatures.[2]

> What then is the soul? According to the Greek philosopher Diogenes, it was Xenophanes who first equated breath with soul, using the word *psyche* with its colourful associations of coolness, bellows and butterfly. Twenty three centuries later, in 1828, Charles Nodier wrote in Paris, 'The different names for the soul, among nearly all peoples are just so many breath variations and onomatopoeic expressions for breathing.'

> *Psyche, anima, atman, savira, semangat, nephesh, otachuk, loakal, tunzi, prana, duk* and *geist* are sacred words used by primal peoples

the world over for the surge of life itself, linguistic cousins of what was called *sawol* by the Anglo-Saxons, *sala* by the Icelandic folk, and eventually, as if stone-polished by the ages, what we now call *soul*.[3]

Indeed, our ancestors believed that the focus of psychic life was in the heart, not in the brain. The heart was more a centre of emotion, love and compassion. It was a centre of thought and imagination, just as it still is for many traditional peoples today, including the Tibetans. Think, for example, of the phrases still used in Christian liturgy: in the Magnificat, 'He hath scattered the proud in the imagination of their hearts'; and in the Collect for Purity in the Anglican Prayer Book: 'Almighty God, into whom all hearts be open, all desires known and from whom no secrets are hid, cleanse the thoughts of our hearts by the inspiration of the Holy Spirit'.[4]

Collins' *Bible Dictionary* defines 'soul' as follows:

soul, a word in the Hebrew Bible with a wide range of meanings. God 'breathed the breath of life' into Adam and he became the 'living soul' (Gen. 2:7). Adam is *living* clay, as opposed to ordinary clay (Gen 3:19). This life principle can ebb and flow; one may fear for one's soul (Ezek. 32:10), risk one's soul (Judg. 5:18), or take one's soul (1 Kings 19:4). 'Soul' may refer to an individual person: Leah bore sixteen 'souls' (children) to Jacob (Gen. 46:18). For a Hebrew, 'soul' indicated the unity of a human person; Hebrews *were* living bodies, they did not *have* bodies. This Hebrew field of meaning is breached in the Wisdom of Solomon by explicit introduction of Greek ideas of soul. A dualism of soul and body is present: 'a perishable body weighs down the soul' (9:15). This perishable body is opposed by an immortal soul (3:1–3). Such dualism might imply that soul is superior to body.

In the NT, 'soul' retains its basic Hebrew field of meaning. Soul refers to one's life: Herod sought Jesus' soul (Matt. 2:20); one might save a soul or take it (Mark 3:4). Death occurs when God 'requires your soul' (Luke 12:20). 'Soul' may refer to the whole person, the self: 'three thousand souls' were converted in Acts 2:41 (see Acts 3:23). Although the Greek idea of an immortal soul different in kind from the mortal body is not evident, 'soul' denotes the existence of a person after death (see Luke 9:25; 12:4; 21:19);

yet the Greek influence may be found in 1 Peter's remark about 'the salvation of souls' (1:9). A moderate dualism exists in the contrast of spirit with body and even soul, where 'soul' means life that is not yet caught up in grace. *See also* Flesh and Spirit; Human Being.[5]

[Among] the early Christian Fathers, there were some who assumed belief in the immortality of the soul. This was defined as an article of faith by the fifth Lateran Council, while the First Vatican Council endorsed the view, in 1870, that souls are directly created by God and infused into the developing embryo.

In traditional forms of prayer prescribed for use in the contexts of dying, burial and memorial, the soul is constantly referred to. Without belief in life after death, Christianity would be a different religion. But few today interpret resurrection in terms of reconstituting cremated corpses, and any other view of resurrection depends upon supposing that personal identity can be guaranteed from one life to the next by continuity of mental characteristics and emotional life. This is precisely what the concept of the soul affirms, and hence belief in the soul would appear to remain essential.[6]

Belief in the resurrection depends on supposing that personal identity can be guaranteed from one life to the next by a continuity of consciousness that makes up the individual soul. This implies a belief that the soul is embodied in life and the Christian sees the resurrection as involving the soul and the body. However, during 'this century advances in evolutionary biology, genetics and neuro psychology along with philosophical analysis of the concept of the person have led many to question the validity of the soul language'.[7]

Many would claim that science has displaced religion as the primary source of authority and meaning, and in doing so has made the notion of the soul redundant. I can only say, as one trained in theology and not in science, that the opposite seems to me to be true . . . cosmology speaks of the soul and we need to hear what is being said. Otherwise the gospel is preached on false premises and meets us only as false selves . . . Cosmology touches the soul. It affects the way we see ourselves, the purpose of our lives and God . . . Matters of the soul have been private or

non-existent, and the soul itself has been reduced to a vague idea
that there might be some fleeting trace of the self which clings on
faintly after death.[8]

Not so very long ago, the word 'soul' was not acceptable in various
intellectual and scientific groups and, although the word is now coming
back into circulation, it still remains practically impossible to define.

In another attempt upon the idea of soul I suggested that the
word refers to that unknown component which makes meaning
possible, turns events into experiences, is communicated in love,
and has religious concern. These four qualifications I had already
put forth some years ago; I had begun to use the term freely,
usually interchangeably with psyche (from Greek) and anima (from
Latin). Now I am adding three necessary modifications. First,
'soul' refers to the *deepening* of events into experiences; second,
the significance soul makes possible, whether in love or in religious
concern, derives from its special *relationship with death*. And third,
by 'soul' I mean the imaginative possibility in our natures, the
experiencing through reflective speculation, dream, image, and
fantasy – that mode which recognises all realities as primarily
symbolic or metaphorical.[9]

The work of scientists like Rupert Sheldrake and Christian thinkers
like Matthew Fox reminds us of two powerful statements by the mystic
Meister Eckhart: '*that the soul is not in the body but the body is in the
soul* . . . what one can know about the soul must be supernatural. It
must be from grace, *for the soul is where God works compassion*'. The
authors are quite clear that 'we are body and soul but spirit is not ours:
it's greater than our bodies and souls. It blows where it wills (John
3:8)'.[10]

The more I meditate on the mystery of the soul, the more I am
aware of the largeness of its mystery. Whatever I write about the soul
is inevitably subjective and personalised, but I find myself very much
in tune with Meister Eckhart who, in the fourteenth century, wrote
these words: 'When God creates the soul, He begets His only-begotten
Son in her, and perhaps before. I say, when God creates the soul, He
creates the soul and begets His only-begotten Son into the soul both
at once in one moment, at the time and above time: thus He pours
His image into the soul.'[11]

Going Forth

The soul remains a mystery. Our searching is an inner journey, linked with our outer journey. I cannot see my soul, yet I feel it will survive as I continue my 'going forth' into the beyond.

5. Growing through Bereavement

The pattern of bereavement is different for every person and it manifests itself through a variety of feelings that differ according to the individual and the length of time shared with the deceased. These may include physical and emotional reactions considered to be normal responses to the loss of a loved one. In addition, for the HIV-positive person there is the experience of stigmatisation. There is not usually the same mutual support for the gay person because of lack of understanding or acceptance of the relationship. People often say, 'Why all the fuss? You've lost a friend, but it's not the same as losing a spouse or a family member.' At this time there is not only disconnection from the partner and his or her family but perhaps also from one's own family if they are not accepting of the partnership.

There are two basic social-psychological processes that describe bereavement – disconnection and reconnection. There is a need to bridge the two as the bereaved person endeavours to grow through the grieving processes. This includes making efforts to preserve the connection with the deceased partner, while at the same time balancing this with activities designed around creating a new life without the deceased. Initially this is done by attempting to preserve a sense of the partner's continuing presence through behaviour patterns and activities that affirm the relationship. This can be through sharing in the partner's care needs during the time of dying, and by becoming involved in HIV/AIDS-related work.

In 1985, Richie was confirmed as being HIV positive and two years later he was diagnosed as having AIDS. Ironically his illness became a very positive part of his life because through it he discovered his ability to write. In 1985, he and I co-founded Streetwise Youth, the first project of its kind in the UK. The aim was to advise, support and counsel young men involved in prostitutional activities at street level. In 1987 Richie co-founded, with Martin Dockerell, Survivors, a male rape support group, again the first such project in the UK.

For me, to share in the caring and the dying of my partner Richie was of great importance. It affirmed, authenticated and enriched our relationship. In the midst of mutually shared pain, there was a great sense of being totally involved in a sacred period in our partnership. It was important for both of us that I was alongside him in hospital as much as possible during his final months. It helped that the care team recognised our special relationship and honoured it by allowing me to assist in his care; to be there when decisions regarding medication and other forms of care were being considered. Nothing was done without our mutual consent. Richie made it quite clear to all concerned, even though he did not make a living will, that I was to be his spokesperson. This was made all the easier by the fact that his family accepted our partnership.

Once Richie had made the decision to receive no further aggressive treatment I became even more involved in his care and spent increasingly more time with him, sometimes in conversation and sometimes in the quietness of just enjoying each other's presence that needed no words. We were there in the truth and in the trust of each other's love. His final days were shared with his family and one or two of our closest friends, all respecting one another's need to have time alone with him.

I will not forget the pain when I realised that Richie was leaving this dimension of life and moving into the mystery of 'the beyond'. As I quietly talked and reassured him of my continuing love and that it was all right for him to let go if he so wished, there was a sense that our love would bridge the gap of separation caused by death. When Richie actually died I did what was most difficult, and yet also sacred. With the nurse I washed his body. Then we prepared him for his funeral. This included dressing him in the clothing he had chosen. It also meant taking off the ring I had given him, which he wanted me to have back, as a 'token of my continuing love and friendship'. I arranged the funeral service, which included a realistically honest reflection on his life. The committal was the most painful stage because it affirmed our physical disconnection.

The limbo of death is certainly a reality. I experienced a kind of numbness as I tried to find my way through a 'cloud of unknowing'. Almost as soon as the funeral was over the family dispersed. For a time afterwards friends did not seem to know how to cope with half the pair of Richie and Bill. This of course is not unique to gay relationships; it also occurs when a spouse dies. For the most part we do not know how to relate to the bereaved person. But it is a particular problem in gay partnerships because often they are not accepted or recognised. In such instances a great deal of time is spent in trying to legitimise and gain social recognition of the significance of the relationship. Acknowledging the partnership (for example, in obituaries) assists the survivor towards maintaining a real connection with the deceased partner by giving him priority of place before, during and after the funeral service. If this does not occur, the psychological distress of bereavement is increased.

In my 'dialogue of grief' with Richie after his death, and with others, I can remember writing letters to him, some of anger and fear, some of love and sheer joy. I would write the letters and then, a few days later, prayerfully burn them. I also remember talking to a trusted friend about my anger and depression. I believe that my reconnection with life began when I realised that, much as I loved Richie, I was also extremely angry with him for having left me. There were times of depression and guilt. I sought the help of a psychotherapist who had also cared for Richie. After a few sessions, the anger and the guilt were understood and I was freed to move on.

This release allowed me to look deep into my recollections of Richie. Through this activity, my appreciation of him grew. It enabled me to give positive thanks for the gift of our relationship. It enabled me to recognise how the wounds of his early life had helped him to become a qualified youth and community worker for the young outcasts of society. If a saint is someone who offers his or her life to the full in caring with and for others, then perhaps Richie could be recognised as such, warts and all.

In the early days I found myself wanting to talk about him and our partnership. To share its ups and downs with others who understood my need to move through the grieving processes. I would often find myself asking him questions, talking to his pictures around the flat, reading his letters and his diaries. At times tears would suddenly well up, especially when I opened a book I had been reading and find in it a note from him expressing his friendship and his love for me, and signed with his sketch of a flower; or I might be walking past an antique shop, fantasising about what we would buy for the cottage. Birthdays and anniversaries brought pain to the fore. My need to have something growing in his memory was met by giving a yellow rose, a symbol of liberation, to be planted in a garden we had both enjoyed. These and many other thoughts and actions helped to release me from the pain of grief, though I suspect that throughout my life these will surface occasionally, but not enough to prevent me from being involved in life.

These various 'rites of passage' were essential, enabling me to re-establish myself as a single person with a future. The most difficult aspect has been to find myself fearful of beginning a new relationship of intimacy, even though I know Richie hoped this would occur.

Then, during the second year after Richie's death, I found myself completing and publishing a book he had started, entitled *Cry Love, Cry Hope*. Doing this has helped me to speak more openly of my feelings with an honesty that allows me to let go and move on in hope. It has also helped me to be aware of the fact that we have unlimited ways of working through our loss.

> We have our bodies with all our vital sensory gifts – movement, touch, sound and vision. We have our innate intelligence and our ability to study, to gain understanding and to seek wisdom. We have our emotions, ranging from apathy and alienation to excitement, love and rapture. We have our deep connection with the infinite or divine, however we conceive it to be. We are equipped to learn, live and evolve.[1]

My personal growth through the wounds of bereavement confirms for me the fact that life initiates death, and similarly that death initiates life.

6. Hope of Life Beyond

Now we see only reflections in a mirror, mere riddles, but then we shall
be seeing face to face. Now I can know only imperfectly; but then I
shall know just as fully as I am myself known. (1 CORINTHIANS 13:12)[1]

Although I have not had a near-death experience, my overview
of the world's faiths suggests they have universally counselled
humankind to keep death in mind if we are to live our daily lives and
our daily dying fully. The question often asked is: What light does the
near death experience (NDE) throw upon the belief in life after death?
The fact that these experiences occur on a vast scale is not in doubt. The
phenomenon has been described in the pioneer writings of Raymond
Moody and Elizabeth Kübler-Ross, while Kenneth Ring quotes from
the Gallup poll '... that somewhere between 35–40 percent of those
who come close to death could report NDEs'.[2] This would, as he says,
represent about eight million adults in the United States alone. We can
assume that millions more will have NDEs in the future, owing to the
highly developed methods of resuscitation technology now available.

Tom Harpur writes: 'According to the International Association for
Near-Death Studies, "An NDE may occur when a person is considered
clinically dead, or even to one not close to death but who is under
some biological and/or psychological stress. Somehow, the experience
appears to be a biologically-based trigger for a spiritual event." '[3] My
personal feeling is that such events are spiritual, if we understand, as I
do, that a spiritual event-experience is something indefinable that places
one outside oneself.

Carol Zaleski finds amazing parallels between the experiences of
medieval saints, mystics and also ordinary people, and those relayed on
talk shows or in the books of the NDE researchers today. But she finds
some remarkable differences too: '... gone are the bad deaths, harsh
judgement scenes, purgatorial torments, and infernal terrors of medieval
visions; by comparison, the modern other world is a congenial place, a

39

democracy, a school for continuing education and a garden of unearthly delights'.[4]

Today we are becoming more aware, and indeed accepting, of this phenomenon through the pioneering work of such as Drs Moody and Kübler-Ross, as well as the research and publications of the International Association for Near-Death Studies (IANDS) and the work of many other writers on this subject (see Further Reading).

The essence of a near-death experience is a completely changed state of consciousness in which the person is aware of the self becoming less physical, of floating into other spaces and sometimes of not wanting to return to the physical state of this life. Often the return to this life is made in order to complete something or to help others who are in need, maybe a family member or a close friend, or it may be to complete some work. More often than not the person returns with a greater sense of tolerance, empathy and loving concern, and a wider openness to other religions, without losing their own denominational or faith allegiance. The most important factor is that there is usually a loss of the fear of death, linked to an increased commitment to and understanding of others. Whatever our views, this experience radically changes the mental and spiritual perspective. As life takes on a new meaning, the concept of growth transcending material satisfaction and life in this dimension is more highly valued than before, reminding us of Wordsworth's view that 'We are greater than we know'.

In *Life after Life*, Raymond Moody has sifted out from a mass of anecdotal material the fifteen most frequently occurring elements in accounts of NDEs and placed them in chronological order. Kenneth Ring has made a similar study:

> I intentionally placed these accounts in a certain sequence to try to bring out this sense of progression. In recalling the features of the core NDE, we should be mindful of its developmental aspects as well.
>
> And so we remember (1) the incredible speed and sense of acceleration as one approaches (2) the light that (3) glows with an overwhelming brilliance and yet (4) does not hurt one's eyes. We remember that one feels in the presence of the light (5) pure love, (6) total acceptance, (7) forgiveness of sins, and (8) a sense of homecoming; that (9) communication with the light is instantaneous and non-verbal and that the light (10) imparts knowledge of a universal nature as well as (11) enables one to see or understand

his entire life, (12) it is clear what truly matters in life. We also remember that one may be aware of (13) transcendental music, (14) paradisiacal environments, and (15) cities of light as one progresses further into the experience. And that, finally, (16) once having encountered the light, one yearns to remain forever.[5]

Near-death experiences are certainly comparable with other types of spiritual awakening experiences. I would define a true spiritual experience, whatever the releasing mechanism, as anything that takes one out of oneself. This leads me to suggest that it may sometimes be as a result of these experiences during the last days of their illness that dying people have requested an end to further aggressive treatment. Such a request may have been made easier by the experience, especially if the person's anxiety, anger or fear has been released, allowing him or her to flow into the light with a peace that contains all understanding. Ring suggests that the ' . . . qualities of the light somehow infuse themselves into the core of the experiencer's being so to lead to a complete union with the light. In apparently the sense in which medieval theologian and mystic Meister Eckhart spoke of man becoming God, NDErs may experience this merging of their own individuality with the divine'.[6]

Clearly the near-death experience is essentially a spiritual one, serving as a catalyst for a spiritual awakening and development towards further growth. No one who has had such an experience seems to be aware of how long it has lasted. However, it seems clear that the nature of near-death experiences is in accord with a general spiritual rather than religious orientation towards life. Ring has summarised the seven essential elements of spiritual development through near-death experience. They are:

1) A tendency to characterise oneself as a spiritual rather than a religious per se.
2) A feeling of being inwardly close to God.
3) A de-emphasis of the formal aspects of religious life and worship.
4) A conviction that there is life after death, regardless of religious belief.
5) An openness to the doctrine of reincarnation (and a general sympathy towards Eastern religions).
6) A belief in the essential underlying unity of all religions.
7) A desire for a universal religion embracing all humanity.

This suggests that, if the essential Me is spiritual and continues to grow beyond the grave, this can only be so because there is life after this life, reached through dying to this life.[7]

Some other writers' comments are relevant here. For example, Harpur quotes Judith Miller: 'We are no closer to answering the basic questions of the afterlife now than we were thousands of years ago when it was first pondered by ancient man'.[8] Zaleski writes: 'We may find no difficulty in respecting the testimony of those whose lives have been transformed by a near-death vision, but we can verify these discoveries only if, in some sense, we experience them for ourselves'.[9]

Harpur also quotes Carl Jung, who says: 'What happens after death is so unspeakably glorious that our imaginations and our feelings do not suffice to form even an approximate conception of it'.[10]

I have an inner knowing that there is life in the beyond of this life. In the present dimension life is a mystery, therefore how much more of a mystery is life after death, nurtured by the hope of millions of people of all faiths and of none. Intuitively I sense that death is not the end, rather the entrance into a mystery beyond our comprehension. It is always risky to generalise, but it is probably sufficient to say that for most of us who do believe in the afterlife, the shape is unknown, yet there is a sense of something beyond this life. Today's search for the truth about the hope of life beyond the grave, nurtured by people's search through previous centuries, may lead only to a mystery that is not to be totally unveiled, but this does not stop us from knowing that life beyond death is revealed by the resurrection and all that it means.

A popular reading requested at funerals and memorial services is part of a sermon preached by Canon Scott-Holland. He is a priest who is very aware of the finality of death, of life as we experience it, yet he is equally confident of the 'ongoingness' of life into the mystery of the resurrection of Jesus, drawing all humankind into the very soul of God. It seems to me that whatever else death may be, it is certainly about ultimate change. The experiences of the incarnation, transfiguration, resurrection, and ascension of Jesus seem to confirm this fact. I suspect that we shall only know the truth when we ourselves have flowed into the mystery labelled death. Yet the idea of an afterlife persists and is encouraged by accounts of near-death experiences. These support a belief in reincarnation, held by Hinduism, Buddhism and other Eastern faiths.

I once witnessed a dying person having a conversation with someone I could neither see nor hear. The question that comes to my mind in such cases is: Is this person hallucinating because of various changes in the body and mind or is he or she really in touch with someone who is dead? I have noticed that a person who is full of anger, and anxiety and fearful of dying, after seemingly having been in touch with someone will become more peaceful and ready to continue his or her journey into the mystery of the beyond. I believe that each person knows from within whether he or she is dying, even though this may not be explicitly discussed. Often the silence of our quiet attentiveness will allow the person to recognise, accept and perhaps discuss his or her dying, when ready to do so.

Dying persons can not only teach us about the process of dying, they can also show us how to live in such a way that, when our time comes for dying, we shall have no unfinished business left behind. I have sensed through each person's dying that there is no afterdeath, only afterlife to be lived to the full.

Elizabeth Kübler-Ross believes that 'Death is the final stage of growth'.[11] I am not so sure about this. I have a gut feeling that growth continues as we move from in-time to out-of-time. I ask myself whether, in dying, we are perhaps being caught up in the mystery of our continuing evolution. It suggests to me that the resurrection and the idea of reincarnation are saying something similar and yet in a different way. Clearly they are both suggesting that death is not final but, like birth, a great act of change through growth.

I cannot judge from a theological point of view, but I believe that reflections on life-after-death are incarnational. To say that 'God was in Christ' is to say that the embodiment of God is in Christ in ourselves and that therefore a relationship is created that is not only significant to God, but also to the human spirit. Is this not borne out for us when the Christian faith proclaims that we are always, in life and death, in God's presence, in whom we live, love, move and have our being – warts and all? *Psalm 139*

It seems to me that the Christian doctrine of survival, of life-after-death, via the resurrection, depends on God's personal blessings of original love and the relationship this nurtures. This suggests that we are seeded in God and born into the dimension of being that we might journey through the gateways of death into the mystery of all creation. To be baptised into the Christ-mystery is to be baptised into the mystery of the resurrection, the new life beyond this dimension of being into the ultimate mystery. Survival after death must be firmly rooted in our awareness of the world as 'the body of Christ', for Christ embraces every dimension of life in this world and in any other world after death. Of life beyond death, Blue writes, in his introduction to the book *Beyond Death*:

> I think the only evidence for it, convincing evidence, is the evidence you provide yourself. In other words you have to *become* your evidence. You can talk glibly about the beyond-life, for and against, until the cows come home, but only when you invoke it and allow it to work on you and you see what it makes of you, only then is it convincing. It is only then, as it were, things turn inside out, and that you find yourself not using it, but *it* using you.[12]

In the midst of life, we are surrounded by death, and in the midst of death we are surrounded by life. Without our daily lives being nurtured through our daily dying, life would be non-existent. Life and death nurture each other and help us grow into the fullness of our potential as we journey through and into the beyond of this life.

7. Rites of Passage: One

The soul is the world within and it is to this inner world that ritual relates. (JAMES ROOSE-EVANS)[1]

Whether we are aware of it or not, routine shapes and regulates our lives. It arises from many sources and activities: through natural and surrogate families, partners, friends and colleagues; through school, college, university, workplace and leisure; and through the church, temple, synagogue or mosque. The routine of the natural world can be seen in the different seasons of the year. To live without routine is to live without a pattern, however fluid, which can nurture our life's journeying.

Some lives are a mixture of routine, rite and ritual. I believe my life to be of this kind, as my average day clearly shows:

5.30– 6.00	Early morning ablutions
6.00– 8.00	Quiet time of reading
	Celebration of Eucharist–ritual
8.00– 9.00	Breakfast, reading the papers, housework
9.00–13.00	Office work, meetings, visiting
	Funeral or memorial service–ritual
13.00–14.00	Lunch, TV news, relaxing
14.00–17.00	Seeing people, meeting, visiting
17.00–18.00	Quiet time, maybe a nap
18.00–22.00	Unstructured
22.00–23.00	Winding down, lights out

The routine will differ on Sundays and when I am away.

A routine can be identified if we take time to look at and assess what we have been doing. For instance, if we look at an event such as a dinner party; there are the invitations, the event itself and the clearing up afterwards. Similarly, we can recognise a routine in relation to a funeral or a memorial service: there is the notification of death, the

45

coming together to arrange the service, the actual service and the gathering afterwards to share memories and offer support.

A rite is a ceremonial act or series of acts with a prescribed form of words, and sometimes music, for specific events. These become formalised through a system of ritual or ceremonial acts or actions. Such events include baptism, puberty, marriage, ordination, profession of vows, initiation, funeral/memorial services – all can be embraced by the term 'rites of passage'. This term was first coined by the French anthropologist Arnold van Gennep in 1909. In defining rites of passage, he observed that they have three characteristic phases: separation, transition and incorporation. In the case of dying, these phases take the following form:

Separation begins when the ill person accepts the fact that he or she is now involved with a life challenging (terminal) illness. Also, those who are alongside are forced to recognise the beginning of a separation process, culminating in the person's death.

Transition means moving into the beyond for the person who has died and a disconnection for those who will mourn and grieve their loss.

Incorporation occurs when the bereaved partner, family and friends accept the end of their former relationship roles to the deceased and are able to reconnect with society.

Life is full of rituals, even though we may not regard them as such. For example, love making, pregnancy and birth, baby feeding at regular intervals, taking treatment or medication at prescribed times – all these are a form of ritual. In addition, there are:

Daily rituals – the morning constitutional, the journey to and from work, jogging or going to the gym, watching a regular TV programme.

Weekly rituals – sporting events, music or theatre, evening classes, religious worship.

Seasonal rituals – Christmas, Easter, holidays, spring and summer festivals.

Religious rituals – baptism, confirmation, bar or bat mitzvah, marriage, religious profession, ordination, consecration, funerals, memorial services.

Life can be seen as a series of rituals, leading us towards the 'letting go' ritual prior to the approach of death.

I believe that a Christian minister must be ready to offer any of the sacraments which may be requested. The dying person who asks, for example, for the rite of baptism, may or may not have been baptised already. Conditional baptism can often fulfil a need. I offer this sacrament because it helps. The other approach – 'You will go to hell if you do not repent and be baptised' – I believe to be religious blackmail.

There may be a request for confirmation too. In such a case it is important to find out whether the applicant understands what is being asked for. A phone call to the appropriate bishop is normally responded to quickly and he will usually come in episcopal vesture. This is often very important to the person being confirmed. Confirmation may be followed by holy communion, depending on the physical state of the person, concluding with an episcopal blessing. It is amazing what the presence of a bishop may do. 'I didn't think he would come for me' is a common response.

The ritual of anointing with the sign of the cross on the hands, feet, torso and forehead is occasionally – though, in the case of Roman Catholics, almost always – asked for. Another request may be for the sacrament of reconciliation and, for some, this is an important part of the process of letting go into the peace that contains all understanding.

The marriage ceremony is sometimes requested by the dying person in order to make his or her cohabitee 'respectable'. This can be done under the Marriage (Registers) General Act, along with an Archbishop's special licence. In the Church of England this may take some time, but the registrar is always on call and able to come at short notice. The licence allows for the minister to receive vows if this has been arranged beforehand. I remember sharing a wedding service and later watching the bride feed her husband champagne from a spoon. The hospital team assured their privacy. A few hours later the husband died in his wife's arms.

Once in a while a request is made for the blessing of a same-gender partnership as an authentication and affirmation of a love shared over the years. I believe there is no biblical injunction against the blessing of a friendship or exchanging rings of friendship.

In their book *Rituals for Living and Dying* Feinstein and Mayo inform us that:

Ritual and rites of passage are traditionally among the most powerful culturally sanctioned vehicles available for exerting influence. They are social inventions for instructing the human spirit on its journey into the world. They transmit the combined wisdom of previous generations and are built on the promise that future generations can derive the lessons of painful experiences without having to repeat them. Rituals, like myths, address (1) our urge to comprehend our existence in a meaningful way, (2) our search for a marked pathway as we move from one stage of our lives to the next, (3) our need to establish secure and fulfilling relationships within a human community, and (4) our longing to know our place in the vast wonder and mystery of the cosmos.[2]

All societies have developed forms of ritual, both secular and sacred, and many have become an essential part of the fabric of culture and faith. Unfortunately, many of these rituals have become fossilised, with no growth or change being allowed, and have not developed new signs and symbols to take account of evolving life, as we live in the present and on into the beyond.

Transition rituals emerge according to need and situation. Some are totally new, others are adaptations of traditional ones, or a combination of old and new. New rituals evolve through the wishes and needs of the individual or the group. In my experience, many young people who are dying as a result of HIV viral infection wish to design their own funeral or memorial services; it is their way of remaining in control of their life and, more importantly, their dying. It is an affirmation that he or she has lived, has loved and continues to have hope in the future. At its best the funeral or memorial service represents a living tapestry of the person's life. My own experience confirms that when individuals are entrusted to create their own ritual they sparkle with life. I have seen such people grow and I have recognised a spirituality that is not institutionalised, one that is open to the mysteries of life and death. 'As Tom Driver has written: "A ritual grows as we grow. What we learn by doing ritual is not only the ritual and how it has been performed before. We discover how to do it the next time." '[3]

Every time I am involved in the creation of a funeral or memorial service I am learning how to be flexible, how to shape the contents of the service to the wishes of the person who has died and the chief mourners. This is of great importance if the service is to flow naturally and be symbolic of the person whose service it is. 'A ritual is like a door in a wall which leads us into a secret garden'[4] – into the beyond.

I am not aware of any mandatory religious or universal ritual relating to death, only that there are different kinds of funeral and memorial services. There are funerals for the stillborn, for children, for young people and for senior citizens. The timing of the funeral will be guided by culture and tradition, by the distances people have to travel and by climatic considerations. Of paramount concern must be the wishes of the partner and the chief mourners. Sometimes the funeral belongs to the immediate mourners, while a memorial service is held for the wider circle of those who grieve. Occasionally the funeral and memorial are linked within one service. Whatever the type of the funeral/memorial service, it should have an appropriate content. It should enable the person whose service it is to be recognised as the person he or she was. We do a disservice to them when we beatify a person; we all have vices as well as virtues.

Ritual has the power to release emotions which need to be liberated, thereby enabling the grieving process to begin. It brings people together in their pain and vulnerability, and their confusion; it has the power to lead us into the inner realm of the psyche and ultimately to that of the soul. James Roose-Evans, in his book *Passages of the Soul*, reminds us that 'ritual works on two levels, that of the psychological and that of the spiritual, and sometimes both coincide. A ritual can resolve, at a deeper level than the intellect, some inner conflict, thereby releasing the individual from a psychological block.'[5]

Ritual marks a transition from one way of being to another. The funeral/memorial service signifies that the person we have known is dead, has moved on from life to death. Certainly a physical separation has taken place. Yet I believe that if we have cared, loved and hoped with the deceased person, we remain linked to them. This is because we are part of the invisible fabric of each other's friendship. The death of someone close demands a release of ourselves into the beyond. Through the ritual of a sensitively offered funeral/memorial service the way will be opened. From my own experience, I share the view expressed here:

> The great death rituals enable the bereaved to return to life and to adjust to the absence of the loved one and, at the same time, enable the soul of the deceased to go on its way. Even on a psychological level we have to learn how to let go of the one who has died. In the Saxon Wicca ritual *Crossing the Bridge at Death*, the priest says these words: "We gather here to say farewell to a

49

friend who must travel far. There is a reason for being here in this world and this life. There is a reason for leaving when the purposes of this life are done. The soul must journey beyond to pause, to rest, to wait for those who are loved. For the world beyond is a land of eternal summer and of joy, far from the cares of this world, with happiness and youth anew". The priest then places on top of the coffin three evergreen boughs and continues: "As the evergreen does grow and prosper both in summer and winter, year after year, so also does the soul continue from life to life, growing ever stronger, wiser and richer." [6]

Although there are many ancient and modern rites of passage, we have very few that enable the bereaved person to recover a full life. We need new rituals that will empower the person to move through his or her grieving. Similarly we need rites of passage designed to help us cope with grief-triggering anniversaries and ones that will enable us to cope with other forms of loss.

Ritual has the ability to connect our individual experiences with the personal, communal and universal experiences of humankind. It is through what we might characterise as a 'This is Your Life' service that we are fulfilling a need. 'John X. Harriot, in one of the last pieces he wrote for *The Tablet* spoke of the need for "rites that reflect and express realities as they are experienced now, and the insight of our own times, not a regression to past ages".[7]

The recognition of rites of passage is essential to life being lived to the full. I would suggest that without rituals we would be existing among the living dead. Rituals which accompany our rites of passage have the energising power of focusing our lives and nurturing our souls. These rituals enable the release of words and feelings we find difficult to explore as we attempt to express the almost inexpressible pain of grief in our lives.

In most religious cultures funeral rites enable those who are dying to make a rite of passage that is intended to aid the psychic and spiritual welfare of the soul.

The Egyptian and Tibetan 'books of the dead' are venerable proto-types in preparing people to encounter the final mystery of their lives. The Egyptian *Rev Nu Pert Em Hru* (Chapters of Coming Forth by Day) dates back to about 1600 B.C. and is a collection of texts that contain formulae, prayers, hymns, and descriptions of the 'Fields of Peace' in the afterlife. The eighth century B.C. Buddhist

Bardo Thodal (the *Tibetan Book of the Dead*) offers guidance at the time of death and in the after-death state . . . The *Bardo Thodal* teaches the dying to face death calmly and with a clear mind, able to transcend bodily suffering and infirmities with a trained intellect directed towards transcendence. Similar books exist in the Hindu, Islamic, and Mesoamerican literature, each reflecting a different mythology concerning death. The European parallel to these works is a medieval collection of literature known as *Ars Moriendi*, or *The Art of Dying*.[8]

Today there are works that can be placed in the same tradition as these ancient and medieval books; examples are *Sadhane – a Way to God*, *Rituals for Living and Dying* and *Passages of the Soul*. There are also numerous books available on how we can turn our fears of dying and death into an affirmation of life, pointing us towards an ongoing future as we flow into the mystery of the beyond.

It seems that within the desert faiths – Judaism, Christianity and Islam – their rituals for the dying and their funerals are intended to unlock the mysterious gateway into the beyond. They remind us that ritual is a lived and living story, not a set formula, in the way that their funeral rites reflect the central beliefs of each faith.

For the Christian, belief in the awesome mystery of the immortality of the soul and the resurrection of the body is central. The prototype for this firm belief is the life, the dying, the death and the resurrection of Jesus-the-Christ. For Christians this is a true parable of the meaning of life; it is a factual drama and a statement that our dying leads to life eternal.

It is remarkable how many similarities there are amongst the rites of the various faiths relating to death and funeral and bereavement practices. Most of us would think otherwise, believing, perhaps, there were no points in common either historically, doctrinally or resulting from origin. However, this clearly shows that people are very much alike at this most stressful period in their lives.

The *Tibetan Book of the Dead*, or the *Bardo Thodol*, is a kind of training manual in 'dying'. Its instruction is of a verbal kind, in which the individual 'learns to die', thereby empowering their true self, the soul or vital force to be strengthened by spiritual exercise. The book was written to counteract the unwillingness of men and women to seek liberation for their souls. It is intended to show a way out of the vicious circle of death and rebirth. In Jung's words, 'it is an initiating process whose purpose is to restore to the soul the Divinity it lost at birth'.

Tibetan Buddhism sees our existence as divided into four realities: life; dying and death; after-death; and rebirth. These are what are known as the Four Bardos:

> the natural bardo of life spans the entire period from birth to death ... the best time to prepare for death by becoming familiar with the teaching and stabilizing the practice. ... The painful bardo of dying lasts from the beginning of the process of dying right up until the end of what is known as the 'inner respiration'; this, in turn culminates in the dawning of the nature of mind, what we call the 'Ground Luminosity' at the moment of death. ... The luminous bardo of dharmata encompasses the after-death experience of the radiance of the nature of mind, the luminosity of 'Clear Light' which manifests as sound, colour and light. ... The karmic bardo of becoming is what we generally call the Bardo or intermediate state, which lasts right up until the moment we take on a new birth. What distinguishes and defines each of the bardos is that they are all gaps or periods in which the possibility of awakening is particularly present. ... [We all] face two causes of death – untimely death and the other through exhaustion of one's natural lifespan.[9]

> The bardo of dying falls between the moment we contract a terminal illness or condition that will end in death, and the ceasing of the 'inner respiration'. It is called 'painful' because if we are not prepared for what will happen to us at death, it can be an experience of tremendous suffering.[10]

> The process of dying is explained in considerable detail in the different Tibetan teachings. Essentially it consists of two phases of dissolution: an outer dissolution, when the senses and elements dissolve and an inner dissolution of the gross and subtle thought states and emotions. But first we need to understand the components of body and mind which disintegrate at death.[11]

It is my hope that this book will, in some way, assist many people throughout the caring professions to recognise the need for spiritual awareness, especially those of us who are alongside the dying and the bereaved. The knowledge that all great spiritual traditions inform us that death is not the end helps us to realise that in life we give rise to death, while in death we give rise to life.

8. Rites of Passage: Two – Those with HIV/AIDS

Today, perhaps more than at any other time, gay people are living in the midst of death and loss, and for many this reality affects everyone to whom they are close. At the same time they are faced constantly with social stigmatisation as a result of being openly gay. They are having to cope with the psychological stress of 'coming out'. Many live with the threat of physical violence from 'queer bashing' and some have been murdered. This possibility has increased since gay men have become more visible and assertive.

I have been for the most part involved in work with members of the gay community, who initially were the most likely to be infected and affected. However, I am not unmindful of the increasing number of other members of society who have and who are continuing to become infected and affected by the AIDS virus. I am thinking of women, whether married, in partnership or single, of women with bisexual husbands/partners, of lesbian women, of children and young people of all and any ethnic origins, and whatever the mode of infection. I suggest that all will go through similar experiences and will need similar services, though unique to each person and situation. The most urgent requirement of all is support, where the person's particular needs will be recognised and addressed.

I feel that the HIV/AIDS crisis is releasing a compassionate and creative approach to dying. The peer groups of young gay men are being forced to care for the dying and the bereaved. For some, their tears are nurturing a hidden creativity and spirituality. Through the pandemic nature of this disease we are being forced to look at new ways of caring for the dying and of perceiving death.

To die of cancer does not carry the stigma of HIV/AIDS, yet it is clear that anyone affected by this life-threatening viral infection will find that close friends and others avoid them through a sense of fear or of helplessness. For some there may be a sense of guilt, while others simply do not know what to say or how to cope, hence they feel embarrassed. However, to die as a result of HIV viral infection can often mean dying alone, as lepers once did, for fear of what the family and neighbours might think if the truth were revealed. Those living with HIV/AIDS are therefore facing two deaths:

- Coming out and facing the truth of their lifestyle may for some be linked with shame and guilt, and also with rejection by their families, their church and society. Some even have to 'die' to these groups in order to live the truth of who they are becoming.
- The consciousness of impending death and how that may take place is heightened by the fear of aloneness, pain, rejection, disfigurement, loss of bodily and mental control and a growing sense of uselessness.

For children, the death of a relative as a result of HIV/AIDS may be even more difficult, particularly if they have no outlet for their grieving. They may sense the presence of a secret concerning the death of their father, mother, older brother or sister, or favourite uncle, but they know they cannot ask questions.

Sometimes a young child may not be allowed to attend the funeral of a member of the family or a close friend. Usually this is because the parents are trying to protect the child. I remember being involved with a family whose son was dying as a result of HIV infection. He was being looked after at home. Whenever the parents were discussing the illness, however, if his adoring seven-year-old sister, Mary, entered the room, the conversation was changed immediately. This was noticed by the child. When her brother died she was not allowed to see him or say goodbye and was not allowed to attend the funeral. Six months later, Mary, who had constantly been top of her class, began truanting from school; at the same time she became very kind and helpful at home. Eventually Mary broke down. She felt it was her fault that her brother had disappeared so suddenly. No one had realised that Mary was mourning her brother. Finally she was allowed to visit her brother's grave and take him flowers; her tears seemed to flow into eternity. Eighteen months later Mary was back at the top of her class.

The stages of grief – numbness, longing, disorganisation of the mind, depression and eventual recovery – are different for everyone. The resolution of grief requires identification of the experiences that allow a relationship to be completed or concluded, then the living are able to 'let go' of the dead, knowing and accepting that in one sense they have lost them, while in another they have not. Following the death of a son or daughter who has died as a result of HIV infection, the family may be left with a feeling of guilt and a sense that they failed to save their child from the behaviour or situation they believe to be the prime cause of infection and death.

The death of the partner may disturb the sense of personal security the bereaved person had depended on. Any attempt to move beyond grief by the dependent bereaved person exposes him to a dangerous world with which he has never had to cope because he previously turned to the partner to protect him. Thus he could face a life of endless grief. His dependency-in-life is converted into a dependency-on-grief and may show itself through an endless searching for the missing part of himself represented by the deceased person. The bereaved person may want to share memories and grief with the family of the dead partner, helping to put together within himself the life of the person he loved. However, because of the pain and anger resulting from their loss, family members may blame the partner for their son's infection and want no further contact with him. This experience of ostracisation after death makes HIV/AIDS different from other fatal illnesses. It may leave the bereaved partner with the legacy of a hostile family.

The nature of each person's relationship to the deceased will affect the process of bereavement. The loss of a dependent or ambivalent relationship may cause intense grieving of a kind that is difficult to resolve. Survivors of marriages, of long-term partnerships, or parent–child relationships that were highly adversarial may have difficulty in accepting the valued aspects of the dead person's life. Ambivalence in a relationship contaminates the grieving process with self-reproach for negative feelings experienced earlier towards the deceased.

HIV/AIDS illness intensifies the sense of helplessness, of hopelessness and of guilt. This is because it reminds the partner of the dying person of what they perceive as the ultimate failure of their caring efforts. These emotions can in turn lead to anger expressed through rejection of the dying person – 'Why are you leaving me?' – or in more covert ways, when it causes additional pain to someone who wants to be able to die with dignity and in peace. These complex and ambivalent feelings then infiltrate and confuse the grieving process. Those who have been exposed to situations of this nature can experience intense, unresolvable grief after the loss of a partner. The lost relationship may have been overtly healing of past wounds through the provision of the single experience of being loved and supported. On the other hand it may be a fostered dependence compensating for a missed early experience of secure family life.

A survivor of a gay relationship may be left with:

- Feelings of social ostracism, real or imaginary.
- Fear of stigmatisation because of the family secret.
- An ambivalent feeling towards partners.
- The desire to blame someone.
- Anxiety about their own possible infection by the partner or others.
- Guilt about having, perhaps, infected the deceased.
- A feeling of failure in the relationship which pushed the partner to seek other sexual contacts to find satisfaction elsewhere.

Post-bereavement losses may include:

- The loss of mutual family connections.
- The loss of the joint home because of the partnership having no legal standing or any religious sanction.
- The loss of friends who do not know how to cope with the single person.
- The withdrawal of friends, especially those who are, or fear they may be, HIV positive, the death having reminded them of their own dying state.

Much of my work as a minister comprises officiating at funerals and memorial services for members of the gay community who have died as a result of HIV infection. When a person dies certain requirements have to be met. These are, I believe, further complicated if the person has died as the result of this infection and is survived by a partner. While some families have no difficulty, others have a great many problems: they have lost a family member; parents do not expect to bury a son or a daughter; they are fearful of the social stigma that may result from a member of the family dying of an opportunistic infection; they may be fearful of the neighbours knowing that their son was gay and living a gay lifestyle; they are not sure how to treat the partner – how to introduce him to other members of the family, and whether they should allow him to organise and/or attend the funeral.

Often there is no consideration of the survivor's feelings, as there would be if the partnership had been heterosexual. Not only does the partner have to cope with his loss, he is, more often than not, left without the support needed by anyone in grief. This may be compounded if he is also infected and perhaps suffering the effects of multiple loss.

It may be helpful to summarise some of the difficulties which may arise with regard to funerals for those who have died of an opportunistic infection related to AIDS. For those involved in nurturing the pastoral relationship, it is essential to know:

- Who the most significant person is in the deceased person's life so that instructions can be taken from him or her.
- How to cope with the family attempting to meet the needs of the deceased person and his or her biological parents, parental figures or guardian.
- How to reconcile any difference between the surviving partner and the deceased partner's family.
- How to cope with any suggestion of banning the partner and friends from the funeral.
- How to assist the bereaved partner before and after the service.
- How to follow up with ongoing pastoral care.
- How to be sensitive to the tensions between different relationships and competition between them.

The arrival of HIV/AIDS has created an intimate connection between love-making and death-making. Death-making is exposing young men to the reality of death, the ultimate letting go of a process that may also release a great amount of creativity and sheer honesty. Many design their own funerals. By doing so they are affirming and authenticating their lives. 'I am what I am' provides the last opportunity for the individual to affirm his own truth as a person and as a member of the gay community. The family may be very confused and may not know how to cope with either his honesty, his dying or his community.

Creating one's own funeral service is part of being in control of one's dying. Any service that results will not only be a mourning but also a celebration of a life lived to the full, rejecting the popular notion that HIV/AIDS is a punishment from God. Because of the Church's attitude towards gay people many do not want a traditional funeral or requiem. But in my experience, these same men are *spiritual*, though not 'religious' in the usual sense of the word. I always encourage the making of both a will and a living will, and the appointment of one or two executors who they feel confident will carry out their wishes. This is essential because often some member of the family will attempt to take over, for legally they are the person's next-of-kin. If the family are wary of the son's partner or friends, they may take over the organising of the service and perhaps transfer it to their local church or crematorium. It then becomes their kind of service, usually one that is utterly foreign to the young person's wishes, and it can mean the exclusion of the partner and friends. The tragedy is when the family have fallen out with their son and he with them, usually because they could not cope with his truth and he with their rejection. The funeral service should release healing processes that have been blocked by the unresolved pain over the years, whether openly shown or not.

I used to think that the point of a funeral is to enable the living to say their last goodbyes to the departed. It was only recently, when exploring the new forms of funeral being pioneered in London by people with AIDS, that I learned that it could also enable the departed to offer a last goodbye to the living. Many will have seen the BBC TV film *Remember Terry*, a documentary of the last months of a forty-one-year-old actor with AIDS. A larger-than-life character who always liked putting on a show, Terry went out in style, at a funeral he himself had orchestrated. The coffin was brought into the crematorium to a taped recording of 'There's No Business Like Show Business'. BBC presenter Patty Coldwell said Terry had asked her to 'pop backstage' behind the curtain and wave a black-gloved hand as the coffin disappeared from view. The song 'Bridge Over Troubled Water' later reduced everyone to tears, which turned to laughter as the curtains closed to the tune of 'Come to the Cabaret'. This was Terry's last farewell, the Terry they all knew . . . and everyone clapped.

Not all gay funerals are as flamboyant as Terry's, of course. As I watched this BBC film, I saw the value of such a service as clearly demonstrating that even in death the truth shall make you free – boldness liberates.

The idea of the deceased waving goodbye, or at least speaking to the congregation from the coffin, is not unique. It is there in the ancient Greek Orthodox service of burial, when the choir sing on behalf of the deceased, as the mourners come to give a farewell kiss:

> As ye behold me lie before you all speechless and bereft of breath, weep for me, O friends and brethren, O kinsfolk and acquaintance. But for yesterday I talked with you, and suddenly there came upon me the dread hour of death. But come, all ye who loved me, and kiss me with the last kiss . . .

Services may be in a theatrical style but few write the entire funeral script as Terry did. However, it is increasingly common for the dying person to suggest a poem, a reading or a hymn they would like to share with those left behind. One young man, thinking about his own funeral, with some guidance from a nun whose work is with people living with HIV/AIDS, decided on the song made famous by Edith Piaf, 'No Regrets'; then for his father he chose Kipling's poem 'If', which had been important to the father as a soldier in the Second World War; and for his mother he asked for some well-known words of Henry Scott Holland.

'Remember Terry' launched a new funeral tradition amongst London's gay community. Many of these people are not only in the full flush of young adulthood, they are creative people used to taking control of their lives. The funeral has become for them a final statement that they are as much in control of their dying as they were of their living.

I believe it helps if we can see death as the final stage of growth, preparing us to move into the beyond. To meditate upon death is to meditate upon life. A prime example of this for me was the Canadian who introduced himself on television as someone with AIDS, to help provide a name, a face and an identity for this disease. Peter introduced himself as a doctor and also as a patient – a patient with AIDS. During his TV series he described the spiritual experience that inspired the following meditation which he privately referred to as his 'Affirmation'. When asked about his religious beliefs, he replied:

> I've never bought into organised religion. I've always felt that a sense of spirituality is a much more personal thing. I didn't have a formulation in mind of what it was I believed in but I knew that I had some beliefs. I grappled with this over the next six months and it seemed to all come together for me on one perfect spring day when I was at Long Beach on Vancouver Island with some friends. It was warm. The surf was pounding on the sand and I decided to take off on my own for a while. I stood there looking around and thinking, 'How much better can it get than this?'. I wanted to be able to recapture this moment for future reference because I knew that I would be facing some difficult times. I also wanted to get a sense of being able to draw in some of the forces that were around me to help me heal myself. So I climbed up on a big rock and laid down in the sun, closed my eyes, and this is what I came up with.

> *I accept and absorb all the strength of the earth to keep my body hard and strong;*

> *I accept and absorb all the energy of the sun to keep my mind sharp*
> *   and bright;*
> *I accept and absorb all the life force of the ocean to cleanse my body*
> *   and bring me life;*
> *I accept and absorb all the power of the wind to cleanse my spirit*
> *   and bring me strength of purpose;*
> *I accept and absorb all the mystery of the heavens, for I am part of*
> *   the vast unknown.*
> *I believe God to be all these elements, and the force that unites them;*
> *And from these elements I have come, and to these elements I shall*
> *   return;*
> *But the energy that is me will not be lost.*[1]

In my own ministry I have heard many similar powerful statements:

> I would never have missed his dying for all the gifts in the world.
> Even though at times I could hardly hold his emaciated body;
> even though I could hardly contain my own pain, my own dying
> in his dying.

> During the whole period of my friend's dying we grew closer
> together as lovers. We were constantly learning about each other
> – until his last breath – what it means to love and be loved.

> We learned that being alongside each other in partnership was as
> enriching in illness as in health. We learned that being alongside
> each other enriched us more than all our sexual activities, our
> loving expanded to include the wholeness of each other, the whole-
> ness of his dying and my dying in his dying.

> I feel I can say we became more whole, more spiritual through
> our body-mind contacts. As we touched each other's soul, each
> other's uniqueness, each other's mystery, each other's undying love.
> Our loving became the invisible fabric of our lives woven together
> upon the loom of life and death for all time.[2]

These testimonies echo my own thoughts and feelings when I lost my
partner and also many dear friends from HIV infection over these last
fifteen years. Through our tears of loss we are, I believe, saying individu-
ally and collectively, 'Love is the link between life and death, between
death and life. It is the invisible soul of all creation.' I know that I will
not lose the love that has been so freely given to me by both men and
women who have made the pilgrimage into the greater mystery. They

have taken with them all the love I was able to offer. I know their greatest legacy is their love for me, which is now part of the invisible fabric of my soul for all time, nourishing me especially during my most vulnerable times. Love says to each one of us I am in you and you are in me for all time, recalling words from St John's Gospel: 'When that day comes you will know that I am in my Father, and you in me and I in you.' (14:20 REB). It also reminds me that there can be no Kingdom of Love without love first being in ourselves for others. And it reminds me too that he who is in the openness of love, loves me in whatever he sees. 'Whatever this man may live, in truth this man lives in me.' (*Bhagavad Gita*, V1:30)

The gay community have developed rituals which allow public expression of feeling to alleviate their grief and give meaning to relationships lost through death. These rituals create a transitional event. While emphasising the continuity of life, they also express symbolically both the need to hold on and the need to let go. Many gay people have been cut off from traditional religion by condemnation of their sexual behaviour. Out of their personal need new rituals – communal, personal and spiritual – have been and continue to be invented. A kind of 'This is your life' celebration, they fulfil people's needs through funeral and memorial services where balloons are released, symbolising the liberation of the soul, and where there are candlelit processions, conveying the message of light journeying through the darkness.

In 1987, in an attempt to fill the inner emptiness and give meaning to loss, a group of people met in San Francisco to make a quilt in memory of partners, and friends lost through AIDS. Since then thousands of panels have been made, and linked together they have become part of the 'Great Quilt' of the Names Project. Each panel is unique to one person who has died, thus keeping the spirit, and the memory of loved ones alive and assisting the grievers to move through their mourning. The Great Quilt joins all the panels together, providing a reminder of a child, a father, a mother, a partner, a writer, a musician, a priest, a doctor, and so on.

In an age that has lost touch with ritual expressions, especially rites of passage, the rediscovery of their value for recovery from bereavement is of immense importance. Rituals are symbolic of the fact we are all a part of the body, mind and soul of all humanity, past, present and future – and that humanity is linked with the 'all' of creation as the body of the mystery labelled God.

9. World Religions' Approach to Dying and Death

All humans are very much alike and yet unalike at this most stressful time in life. (BILL KIRKPATRICK)

I would suggest that we are fast becoming, if we are not already, a multi-faith country. We should therefore welcome and respect the different attitudes and practices, not only between the various faiths, but also within them. This is why I feel it may be helpful in this book to include an overview of the beliefs and practices of Buddhists, Christians, Hindus, Jews, Muslims and Sikhs in relation to dying and death.

Each faith's answer to the eternal question 'Where do I come from?' can influence the answer to the other eternal question 'What happens after death?' This complex issue is further complicated by the fact that in western and eastern faith traditions these matters are seen quite differently. On this subject Kenneth Kramer writes:

> Each view, however, can be represented as a significant part of a cosmic circle which symbolises the dynamic processes of creation, life, death and rebirth. Each cosmic circle revolves in its eternal cycles of creation, death and re-creation, and beckons the viewer to a deeper understanding of its mysteries. Hidden from full view, the spiritual geometry of each symbolises, in its own fashion, the source of human origins and human destiny.[1]

CHRISTIAN ATTITUDES AND PRACTICES

> In the New Testament teachings about death, at least four key aspects arise: death is a consequence of sin, death is a temporary separation of body and soul, death to sin is birth into eternal life, the dead will be raised and judged at the second coming of Christ.[2]

Prayers for the dead are based on the belief that God has the power beyond the grave to cleanse us of our sins and lift the deceased person into his presence. As death approaches some Christians may wish to have the prayers for the dead said for them, while others may ask for anointing. When death is imminent and if the dying person requests it, a priest or minister will offer communion, which may be shared by others, and together they may also say prayers of commendation.

Both the Roman Catholic and the Orthodox Churches offer the sacrament of healing (formerly the sacrament of the sick), in which the ill or dying person is prayed with, or, if unconscious, prayed over. Traditionally, six parts of the body (eyes, ears, nostrils, lips, hands and feet) are anointed with holy oils previously blessed by the bishop for this purpose. The sacrament is intended to nurture the soul, to give spiritual comfort and to enable the person to meet death calmly and with hope. The Anglican Church also offers this sacrament, if requested, but, in common with other Protestant churches, does not often use it. More frequent is the laying on of hands in prayer.

After death, there are no special requirements, beyond the sensitive preparation of the body for viewing in the chapel or the home, prior to the funeral service. This service may take place in a church or chapel – especially if the person is to be buried there – or in the chapel of a crematorium. The funeral is often for family and close friends. This may be followed later by a memorial service of thanksgiving for the deceased person's life.

If it is a funeral in an Anglican church, the coffin may be brought into the church with prayers the night before, then the next day a simple funeral service may take place. In most instances the coffin is closed, unless otherwise requested. The key part of the Anglican funeral service is the committal. Often the funeral cortège starts from the deceased's home. Afterwards the mourners are usually invited back to the deceased's home for some refreshment and for mutual support and sharing of memories. Today there is no official mourning period or mourning dress. However, within a few weeks, there might well be a service of thanksgiving, which is more of a celebration of the deceased's life, often for those who could not come to the funeral.

The Roman Catholic Church has historically placed more emphasis on ceremony then any other Christian denomination in the West apart, perhaps, from high-church Anglicans who, in some instances, are more inclined towards ritual than their modern Roman Catholic counterparts. Recently, it has become the norm to give thanks for the life of the deceased because it is assumed that he or she is already on the way to heaven. The Roman Catholic Church generally divides the funeral rites into three parts: first the vigil, then the liturgy and finally the committal for burial or cremation.

The vigil is a prayerful watching over the body; this is seen as a rite in itself and as an act of worship by the bereaved. It usually takes place in the church, though it can also be in the deceased's home or in the undertaker's chapel. If it is in the church, this usually occurs the evening before the funeral service. The officiating priest receives the coffin at the church entrance, sprinkles it with holy water and then leads the way into the church's side chapel where the coffin will rest, with three candles on either side. Prayers for the deceased are lead either by the priest or by a lay person if no priest is available. Relations and friends, if they so wish, will read from scripture or say some prayers.

At the funeral itself, the coffin is placed before the sanctuary steps. The chief mourners will have decided whether or not the coffin should be left open. The purpose of leaving it open is to allow for the deceased person's forehead to be signed with the cross, as at baptism. At the Requiem Mass the vestments worn by the priest and the assistants vary in colour depending on conservative or liberal style of worship. They may be the traditional black or the more modern violet or white, the latter symbolic of our resurrection future. Hymns may replace certain liturgical texts, and the priest may offer a homily rather than a eulogy.

Mourners may prefer to have an evening mass, followed by a service the next day consisting only of morning prayer and commendation. If it is a burial, the mourners are invited to sprinkle a few drops of holy water or some earth on the coffin. At a cremation service, the mourners may sprinkle holy water on the coffin prior to the committal signal being given. The ashes may then be buried in a churchyard, using a biodegradable container, or wherever the deceased or their family has chosen. As with most Christian denominations, the mourners usually gather after the service for refreshment and for a sharing of memories and mutual support.

The Greek and Russian Orthodox Churches share similar beliefs about death and bereavement. There is a basic teaching that persons are both soul and body, and in death the two are separated. In the mystery of the resurrection the two come together again; this time, as Saint Paul reminds us, the body is perfect and incorruptible and the human personality is restored.

It is believed that, for the first three days after death, the person's soul hovers near the places he or she has known in life. During these

three days, the mourners' general thoughts are on their relationship
with the deceased, and these thoughts are examined, thereby purifying
the bereaved persons' hearts of any lingering resentment towards the
deceased. They can then in truth and with a clear conscience say to
the soul of the deceased, 'Go in peace'.

The Greek Orthodox service is considerably shorter than that of the
Russian Orthodox Church. The funeral is usually celebrated in a church,
with the coffin left open and with candles placed at the head and feet
of the deceased. The service starts with the priest putting on his stole.
He then recites prayers, either in the home of the deceased or in the
church and later at the graveside. Burial is the usual practice and some
cemeteries have a section especially for Orthodox Church members.
Cremation is relatively rare and an Orthodox priest would not attend
one. In addition to the standard funeral service, an elaborate set of
prayers may be recited by a bishop, at either the funeral or the memorial
service. These will not be said, however, if the deceased has committed
suicide.

For Russian Orthodox Church members there are two principal
funeral rites. There is a short one in the nature of a memorial chiefly
concerned with the souls of the dead generally and there is the full
funeral service for a specific deceased person. There are also special
services for deceased children and for priests. The content of the funeral
service is concerned mainly with the soul and body of the deceased.
Just before the dismissal of the congregation, the priest offers the body
a kiss and each member of the congregation follows suit, led by the
chief mourners. While this is taking place, the lector chants, 'Come,
O Brethren, to give the last kiss to the departed'.

JEWISH ATTITUDES AND PRACTICES

In the Hebrew Bible, the word death is used in at least three ways:
as biological cessation, as a power which opposes God's creation,
and as a metaphor for anything which leads a person away from
God. The emphasis, however, was on the first.[3]

For the religious Jew then, perhaps it can be said there need be
no fear of death. Death is sacred and a natural part of God's
creation. It was, and is, the result of sinful nature; yet, the dead
will be raised again with the coming of the Messiah.[4]

Jewish ideas of what happens to the dead have a long and varied history.

'Early Jewish attitudes towards death did not hint at a return to God and what remained was a "shadow" or "shade", an impermanent residue is *sheol* (probably meaning "underworld" or "non-land" or "unland").'[5] Some believe in hell, for others there is the concept of a resurrection. Among Reform Jews and other similar groups, these ideas have been replaced by the doctrine that the soul is immortal and will eventually attain spiritual ecstasy. 'What unites, or ought to unite, Jews in this country is that they are still labouring under a collective bereavement – that of six million of their kind, many of them close relatives, slaughtered in the most nauseating fashion by the Nazis.'[6]

As death approaches, a rabbi may be called to join the dying person in prayer and to facilitate the recitation of a death-bed confession. When death is imminent the dying person should not be left alone. Those present will join in saying the prayer of 'Justification of Judgement' and when death occurs the 'Declaration of Faith' is said. Immediately after death, health workers should sensitively handle the body as little as possible, except to close the deceased's eyes and mouth, with the jaw being tied closed if necessary. Where possible, the corpse is then placed on the floor and covered in a white sheet. A candle is lit and placed near the head. The Jewish Burial Society will collect the body and perform a ritual wash before burial. Post-mortems are not favoured unless unavoidable. Burial rather than cremation is the norm for orthodox Jews, though some non-Orthodox Jewish communities allow cremation.

Burial is carried out as soon as possible, using a simple coffin. The service takes place in a synagogue, followed by burial in a designated Jewish burial ground. One of the principal mourners offers the eulogy over the coffin as it is lowered into the grave. All males attending a Jewish service should wear a skull-cap, whatever their faith or non-faith. Funerals do not take place on the Sabbath, a day of rest, or other holy days.

After the burial there are three periods of mourning throughout which designated mourners recite prayers three times daily. Mourners also refrain from certain activities during the first seven days. This is followed by a less severe mourning period of thirty days, which concludes the mourning for all except for the children of the deceased who remain in mourning for a year. On the anniversary of the burial a member of the family recites the Kaddish prayer and a reading from the Prophets. They also peruse the Torah (the first five books of the Hebrew Bible) and light the memorial illuminations.

Nowadays those who commit suicide are entitled to equal treatment with those who have died involuntarily. In general, suicides and other transgressions against God's law are not subject to mourning under the full set of rules.

ISLAMIC ATTITUDES AND PRACTICES

For the Muslim, death is a transition from this world to eternity. The purpose of life, according to the Qur'an, is to prepare for eternal life, for 'every soul shall taste death'. In the Islamic faith there is a belief in the Day of Judgement and the stages of life, death and resurrection have no meaning until one completes the full cycle.

As death approaches, family members and other Muslims join the dying person and together they recite verses from the Qur'an. The dying person may ask to be positioned so as to have his or her body facing towards Mecca (in this country, towards the south-east). When death is imminent, the 'Declaration of Faith' is said and the dying person responds, if possible, with 'I bear witness that there is no God but God and Muhammed is his prophet'.

Immediately after death, if health workers or other attendants are not Muslims they should seek permission to touch the body and only then do so with disposable gloves. The body must be handled with great sensitivity as Muslims believe that the deceased soul stays in the body for some time after death, and they further believe that the corpse can feel pain. Soon after death there is a ritual washing of the body by Muslims of the same gender as the deceased. Traditionally this is done by the closest male relative on the father's side.

Muslims are usually buried within twenty-four hours of death. Women do not attend the burial; it is the male members of the family who carry the body either to the mosque or directly to the cemetery where the burial is held and the final prayers said. All should stand as the body (within a coffin or not) is lowered into a deep grave facing towards Mecca.

Islamic law requires friends and relatives to feed the mourners for three days. Following this period, mourners are expected to resume normal life, although a widow traditionally observes the full mourning period of four months and ten days. Forty days after the death a memorial service is held and the period of mourning ends with readings from the Qur'an and a meal.

BUDDHIST ATTITUDES AND PRACTICES

Buddha's teaching about death can be summed up as follows:

> All life is forever vulnerable to suffering; everything is constantly changing; while whatever is born must sooner or later die, there is no fixed self that dies; and as long as one is completely absorbed in grief there can be no release from the fear of death.[7]

> Buddhists believe in reincarnation, but the state of mind and the spirit in which people die is important. To Buddhists, death is the entrance to a transitory state often between one earthly life and the next.[8]

As death approaches, the dying person needs peace and quiet to allow for meditation, as the monk or religious teacher chants passages of Buddhist scripture. This can be done by a fellow Buddhist if a monk or teacher is unavailable.

Immediately after death there are no special requirements relating to the care of the body. Buddhists from different cultures will have their own traditions regarding the care of the body. Local traditions also determine whether the body is buried or cremated. In the UK cremation or burial is equally acceptable. White or black may be worn by the mourners. The person conducting the service usually opens it by referring to the 'passing' of the deceased, at the same time reminding those attending that death is part of the natural order of things. It is all part of the endless life-cycle. During the service the person officiating leads the people in litanies and prayers; there is a blessing of the water and those attending the service assist in the lowering of the coffin into the grave.

The different branches of Buddhism have developed different traditions. Zen Buddhist teaching maintains that death is 'the absolute negation of everything, including itself [and] . . . consists in acquiring a new viewpoint on life and death'.[9] Tibetan Buddhists teach that to understand what happens at death is to become increasingly aware of the total nature of the mind. For them a person's spiritual state when they die is crucial to his or her total liberation. This is why they have no problems with informing the dying person of his or her forthcoming death thereby enabling that person to begin a mental and spiritual preparation for death.

HINDU ATTITUDES AND PRACTICES

Hinduism is a very diverse religion with many differing beliefs and traditions, and a caste system that can seem complex to the western mind. The idea of reincarnation is acceptable to the majority, and as a result their attitude towards death is calm and meditative. Hindus see death as one of the four miseries of material existence, along with birth, disease and old age. They believe that it is the body alone that dies, not the person. Death is seen as ever present, both in the body and in the world, at every moment and the only teacher about death is death itself.

As death approaches, Hindus may receive comfort from hymns and readings from holy books. The family should be present throughout the person's dying. For the Hindu it is important to die lying on the floor with his or her head in line with the earth's magnetic field. If the person dies in bed, he or she is placed on the floor and a candle lit. Immediately after death, if it is an adult male, the most senior male member of the family will wash the body, in line with requirements of traditional practice and caste.

The body is cremated as soon as possible after death. The only exception is for children under three, who are buried. Part of the service will take place at home, where the priest will chant from the scriptures and the chief mourner (usually the eldest son) will perform the rituals. During this time mourners walk round the coffin, which is then closed and taken to the crematorium (or to the cemetery in the case of a child).

After the funeral, mourners and friends return to the deceased person's house and some will stay with the family for a while. The customary period for grieving is between ten and fourteen days, culminating in rituals which enable the deceased person's soul to join their ancestors. There may be further rituals at intervals of one, three, six and twelve months.

SIKH ATTITUDES AND PRACTICES

The Sikh belief is that it is part of God's purpose that we all die. Death is regarded as similar to sleep and of short duration. Individual existence is considered to be the result of a repeated sequence of birth, death and rebirth as the soul seeks spiritual enlightenment. For the Sikh, God is all-pervading and is the source of life. It is believed that a dead person's virtuous deeds constitute a link with those still alive and, together with his words, stand as his true memorial. This is why there is a complete prohibition of any kind of memorial. Prayers for the dead form no part of the Sikh religion.

The dying person may receive comfort by reciting hymns from the Sikh holy book. A relative or any other practising Sikh may share in the reciting of the hymns. It is important that the person should die while speaking the name of God (Wonderful Lord). Some may ask for holy water to be put into the mouth.

After death the attendants should not trim the person's beard or cut his hair. The body should be covered with a plain white cloth. 'The five Ks form an essential part of the dead male's body adornments: the *kaccha*, or knee-length shorts; the *kangha* or small comb which holds in place the *kesh* or uncut hair; the *kara*, a steel bangle; and the *kirpan*, a small sword.'[10] The washing and dressing of the corpse should be done by a member of the same gender.

Cremation takes place as soon as possible after death (unless the law of the land forbids it). Prior to this, a short ceremony takes place in the home, then the body is taken to the crematorium for more prayers. Following the service special food is shared amongst the mourners, symbolising the necessity for ordinary life to continue, although on the actual day of the person's death no cooking takes place at the home.

The day after the cremation the family gathers the ashes for scattering on the surface of a river, or they may be kept until they can be taken back to India. Up to ten days following the cremation daily readings from the scriptures take place, attended by relatives and friends. On the tenth day the eldest son is given a turban as the sign that he is now the head of the family.

This brief introduction to the 'world's sacred traditions' shows that the person who is able to die in a state of spiritual awareness and anticipation, and to feel that they are being reborn, is able to face death with a transformed attitude. This affirms that our daily dying is the nurturer of our daily living. The two bond together as the inner fabric – the soul, if you like – of our lives, helping our continuing transformation, our going forth, into the ultimate mystery.

10. The Funeral Service

In my end is my beginning. (T. S. ELIOT)[1]

I believe the funeral service is as much for the living as for the departed. It is a reminder to us that a human life has ended and that it has made a deep impression on those who are mourning its passing. We are aware that millions of people every day are mourning the loss of someone and at the same time that the funeral we are attending is saying something very significant to us about a specific human life. The main purpose of a funeral is to signify the event of a death, marking the fact that a valuable human life has passed on into the beyond. It also plays an important role in meeting the needs of the mourners. It offers them permission to grieve. It is the last act and a final statement about the deceased.

The funeral service has several distinct aspects:

- The physical aspect – the disposal of the body.
- The social aspect – the need for support for the bereaved at this most isolating of periods in one's life.
- The spiritual aspect – the relationship of the mourners to the current state of the dead person.
- The psychological aspect – liberating the mourners to grieve.
- The economic aspect – awareness of who does what, for whom and at what price.

There are many types of funeral:

- The silent funeral where there is no spoken commendation: it simply begins and ends with prayer.
- The simple service where no tributes are offered except that of silence; it is brought to a close by the person chosen to do so.
- The meditative funeral where, following the main statement, there is time for reflection, with meditative music in the background. The

service is guided by the officiant, who does not have to guide the meditation.

- The church or chapel service conducted according to different beliefs and rites.
- The Anglo-Catholic or Roman Catholic Requiem Mass which can range from the simple to the theatrical (in the best sense of the word).
- The Requiem Liturgy of the Orthodox Churches, which is also theatrical and full of movement, not only of the priests but also of the congregation.
- The cremation service held in a crematorium chapel. If well thought out it can be just as meaningful as one held in a church or chapel. Often there is a service of committal following the main service in church or chapel, usually of short duration.
- The non-religious service, where the minister of any denomination may be asked to lead.
- The burial or cremation where the deceased has stipulated that no service should be held and/or that no one attend the event.

I am in favour of funerals being held in the round, so that mourners may sit or stand around the deceased and touch the person or the coffin. For the bereaved this is their final walking away and the beginning of the healing journey which each needs to undertake.

The idea that children should not attend because it might be painful, or they would not understand, is, I feel, a false one. What is forgotten here is that the parents find it hard to cope with the child's grief alongside their own. They are unable to recognise that children *do* have a sense of what is fitting and can respond honestly when given the opportunity. For instance, eight-year-old John insisted on bringing the family dog to the funeral. Why? 'Because he's part of the family and needs to say goodbye too – then he and I can comfort each other' he explained. Children do understand in their own way. To prevent them attending is to lay the ground for an unhealthy expression of grief at a later date. They have a right to share in the farewells and the corporate grief. For the child or the young person, it is essential that they are part of the service and, where appropriate, that they see the deceased in the open coffin and watch the coffin being lowered into the grave or passing through the doors at the crematorium.

One of the main purposes of the funeral is to help the mourners to release the pain of grief. To imprison the emotions is psychologically harmful. Our emotions should not be feared.

The funeral is a clear expression that life will not be the same. The degree of difference depends upon the closeness of the relationship shared, not necessarily its length. Within this ending is the beginning of various changes needed for the bereaved to reorganise their life and to be reorientated towards a newness of life.

By law the funeral belongs to the next of kin. Unless a will is made by the deceased while of sound mind, the next of kin may legally take over all the arrangements without the surviving partner being involved. Equally there is no guarantee that the dead person's wishes will be carried out. This is why it is essential for the person to make a will, explaining the kind of funeral or memorial service desired. This needs to be supported by executors who the person feels will comply with their wishes as closely as possible.

So far as I know there is no law in the United Kingdom that stipulates: (a) using the services of a funeral director, ordained clergy or any other official to preside at the service; (b) the number of persons who should be present at the service; (c) the use of a specifically licensed building for the funeral; (d) burial or cremation in an official cemetery or crematorium. However, the law does state quite clearly that the next of kin or the person with the full power of attorney is responsible for the procuring of a death certificate, first for the purpose of registering the death, and second, to dispose of the body in accordance with public health regulations and those of the individual cemetery or crematorium.

Being involved with dying persons, especially those between the ages of eighteen and twenty-five, has shown me the value of pastoral care from the time of first meeting the person, which may be anything between three months and two years before his or her demise. To be alongside the person who is dying, to share the bereavement with loved ones, aware that each person will respond in a different way, and to share in the designing of the service and act as a kind of master of ceremonies is indeed a privilege. This also provides a link for those who are bereaved because, today, many people rarely attend religious services except for baptisms, weddings and funerals, and most have only vague memories of church services when at school. Despite this, it is surprising how often the clergy are sought, even if only because it is assumed to be the right thing to do socially. The minister will be there as a guide and comforter to assist the bereaved through their sense of loss and helplessness.

Every funeral should be a service that reflects the life of the dead person, thereby dignifying that life through formal and informal expression, allowing the truth and the humanity of the person to shine through. A funeral is not the time to impose theologically correct statements. It should convey a sense both of mourning and of hope. For this to occur, the putting together of the service calls for attentive listening on the part of the minister so that the different strands of light and dark can be found in the person's life.

Occasionally there is a request for the coffin to remain open during the funeral. However, in the majority of instances the coffin is closed, the chief mourners having earlier placed a flower or some object of significance to the deceased inside. However painful, I believe it to be essential for the chief mourners, and others if they wish, to share in this final act of service and also in the silence prior to the committal, perhaps by throwing some earth or a flower on to the coffin at the graveside, or in a crematorium by touching the coffin during the final piece of music.

Occasionally there may be a request for a video to be taken of the service, perhaps to send to family and close friends who could not attend. Sometimes, too, there is a request that friends and family members act as pall-bearers.

If you wish to bury someone in a local-authority-run cemetery or a churchyard and you want to conduct the proceedings yourself, then you must inform the cemetery officials, or the vicar, giving at least forty-eight hours notice in writing. The request should be signed and include your name and address, and the envelope marked with the words 'Notice of Burial'.

For the burial to take place in a private garden, it is necessary to check out the title deeds of the house for any possible restrictive covenant against doing so. This will cause some difficulty should you wish to sell the home later; if you do so, the ownership may pass to total strangers and their successors who may or may not give you access to the person's grave. Should you wish to exhume the body for reburial elsewhere you will need to obtain a Home Office licence to do so. It is also necessary to have the approval of the local authority's planning department and/or legal department. Once planning permission is given, it is important to obtain a letter, stating that you are not doing anything against the law and that you have a 'Certificate of Lawfulness'. None of these services is free.

If the person has been cremated, the ashes may be interred, scattered or kept somewhere near the home. If they are not to be scattered at the place asked for by the deceased it will then be up to the partner or the executors to decide where. Whether the ashes are interred in a cemetery, placed in a niche in a crematorium, scattered at sea or under a tree or a rose bush, for example, this can take place at any time, with or without a minister in attendance, perhaps accompanied by a traditional or a specially composed prayer. The first thought is often to inter the person in the garden that they created and loved. This is fine until the day comes to sell the house and garden, because the new owners may not afford access; this needs to be considered before a site is chosen. The ashes may be kept indefinitely, so there is no rush to make a decision; yet the longer it is deferred, the more difficult it can become to let go of the ashes and this may hinder the beginning of the healing process.

When the service takes place in a church, it may be followed by committal at the crematorium or in the cemetery. If the deceased was a practising Christian then the body may be received into the church the night before the funeral, with the main part of the service taking place either at the graveside or at the crematorium. This allows for different choices. If the whole service is to take place in the crematorium, it is advisable to suggest a longer period than the allotted time of 20–25 minutes.

The committal may be attended by all or only a few members of the congregation. The chief mourners may wish to attend the committal service in private to allow them space to be on their own in their final farewells. The ritual of the committal service is the final act of letting go and because of this it can be more emotional than all that has gone before. The finality of the service is clearly recognisable. The deceased is seen to be leaving those left, rather than the other way round.

It is an extremely emotional time for some, who cannot bear to see the coffin being lowered into the darkness of the grave or the going forward of the coffin into the place of cremation. Some, therefore, will prefer not to attend the committal service. Not being there softens the reality. Whether or not to attend is a personal choice and should not be dictated by others. Either of these final actions informs us that the person is dead: the lowering of the coffin or its passing through the doors is a re-enactment of the death moment.

The focus of the memorial service, often held several days or weeks later, is generally one of thanksgiving. It also enables those who were unable to attend the earlier service to be present. There can be a great

deal of flexibility with respect to duration, place and structure of the
service and the time of day. It can be held anywhere: the home,
the church, the pub, or wherever seems appropriate for all concerned,
allowing all to reconnect with their own and others' lives.

The funeral has the power of affirming that the person we mourn is
dead, allowing us to 'let go' and to become reconnected to life without
the person's physical presence, thereby leaving space for our continuing
growth through the healing energies of bereavement. The funeral is
the meeting point between the dead and the living, a reminder that
life is for living in the present and that our daily dying will enable us
to live more fully in our 'going forth'.

Commendation and Farewell

We seem to give them back to Thee, O God, who gavest them
to us. Yet, as Thou didst not lose them in giving, so do we not
lose them by their return. Not as the world giveth, givest Thou,
O Lover of souls. What Thou givest, Thou takest not away, For
what is Thine is ours also if we are Thine. And life is eternal and
love is immortal, and death is only an horizon, and an horizon is
nothing save the limit of our sight. Lift us up, strong Son of God,
that we may see further; cleanse our eyes that we may know
ourselves to be nearer to our loved ones who art with Thee. And
while Thou dost prepare a place for us, prepare us also for that
happy place, that where Thou art we may be also for evermore.

(WILLIAM PENN)[2]

11. Co-creating a Service

A ritual involves an offer of one's self: to a deity, to some cause or higher purpose, or to a fellow human being. (JAMES ROOSE-EVANS)[1]

There are three basic components of the service structure – silence, music and words. Each has its place and all may be apportioned according to the wishes of the deceased, if known, or those of the chief mourner(s). Music and words often form the larger part of the service since many cannot bear silence as it tends to reveal the hidden pain.

Music enriches the service, while at the same time saying something relevant, especially if it is appropriate to the deceased person's life. Modern music may be difficult for the older generation and it is helpful to print out the words of any songs in the service programme, and perhaps to read them out: this helps the mourners to see why a particular song has been chosen. (The songs may have been chosen by the deceased themselves.) Contemporary music can be very suitable for the service of a young person. Much of it is beautiful, with thought-provoking lyrics that can be extremely moving. It is out of respect for the deceased that we should do all we can to conform to his or her wishes. Should there be any objection to the music requested by the deceased or their partner, a compromise may need to be made. This might be complicated by the fact that, if there is no will, the family can, in law, claim the right to control the entire service and decide who may or may not attend.

Hymns have a real value by providing for the involvement of the mourners. Some would suggest that they are our sacred folk music; for example, the 23rd Psalm sung to Crimond has become very well known. Some of the services I have been involved in have begun with sacred music, such as selections from various requiems, gradually moving towards modern or pop music as the service draws to an end.

The music for the service may be a mixture of live and recorded music. If the latter is used then a sound system will be required. It is essential that each piece of music to be played is on a separate tape, labelled and numbered in order of play. If live music is requested, whether vocal or instrumental, it helps the performer to have a rehearsal beforehand in the church or wherever the service is to take place. The gift of live music is often more significant if offered by a friend of the deceased, whether a professional musician or not. If the soloist breaks down emotionally this is not to be worried about. (At the beginning of the service I suggest that it is all right to share one's emotions.) Some would believe, as I do, that this may be the greatest gift to the mourners – the freedom to shed tears of grief. To enable the musical aspect of the service to flow smoothly, it is essential that the minister knows who is performing – e.g. organist or soloist – and in what order. The tunes of any hymns or songs chosen to be sung by everyone should be well-known ones.

Flowers have the ability to add a decorative warmth, especially if the place in which the funeral is held is rather stark. Floral tributes as final gifts can be arranged either in sprays or in wreaths of different shapes. Sometimes each person is asked to bring a single flower of their choice or one that symbolises the deceased person. Alternatively, the chief mourner may provide a single flower to be given to each person attending the service. At an appropriate time they will be asked to lay the flower either on the coffin or on a table which may have on it an enlarged photograph of the person, or the flowers might be placed on a green carpet of foliage covering the top of the coffin.

It is important that the funeral director knows what is to happen to the flowers after the service. Usually they are quite willing to deliver them somewhere. Before this is done, the cards accompanying the flowers are given to the person making the funeral arrangements. To people who are on low incomes or state benefits and for whom the purchase of flowers may be too costly, one can suggest the giving of a single flower, which will have as much symbolic value as an expensive bouquet. Sometimes the deceased leaves instructions for the flowers to be given anonymously, for example, to the elderly in hospitals or nursing homes. This is why single flowers or sprays are best.

Forms of tribute other than flowers are increasingly becoming the norm at funerals of young people. Often items of personal significance are placed in the coffin before it is closed. These may include any of the following: a favourite photograph, sealed farewell letters, a favourite or newly written poem. Sometimes these are placed on top of the coffin or on a table nearby. Often the deceased is clothed in his or her favourite clothing, such as jeans, a colourful shirt or sweater, and a comfort toy, like a teddy bear, is placed in or near the coffin.

Such acts personalise the service and give the mourners something tangible to offer as their last gift to the deceased. People may sometimes ask that a rose or a tree is planted, symbolising new and continuing life. Some may request no flowers at all and ask that the money be given to a specific charity of their choice. I remember being involved in the service of a young man who had requested that his coffin be surrounded by tall grass and weeds from the wild patch in his garden. He said that, for him, they symbolised freedom and individuality.

If the deceased person has already designed his or her funeral service, the minister's role is to ensure that these wishes are carried out as requested. This also means that the minister is fully aware of the significance of the service for the surviving partner, whatever the nature of their relationship.

If the person has not made his or her wishes known for the service, then we have to rely on those closest to the deceased to provide the information. We may also be assisted by looking through photo albums or watching a video of the person. Given time and quiet encouragement, a great deal can be revealed and we are able to shape the eulogy and/ or reflections.

The function of the words in the service, whether they are said, sung or prayed, is to put the mourners in touch with the pain of grief and its healing potential. A sensitively honest eulogy is the bridge between the pain of disconnection and the beginning of reconnection with life. A eulogy can be offered by a person who is able to speak from direct experience and knowledge of the life of the deceased, while reflections can be offered by the minister or someone who has not known the dead person. He or she must rely totally on information given by others for the co-creating of the reflections. This enables the minister to speak of the deceased in such a way that he or she is recognised by the mourners. Careful attention must be paid to detail; any slip-up may spoil the service. A mistake, such as using the wrong name, will suggest that the minister has not taken enough care.

In the preparation of the eulogy it is most important for the minister to meet with the bereaved partner, the families and the extended family members of friends in order to try to understand the depth of their loss. We shall do this better if we have come to terms with our own losses and bereavements because this will help us to empathise more effectively with the grief of the bereaved. If I have never met the deceased, for the reflections to be real I know I must listen attentively to the bereaved to gain a real awareness of the dead person's life and character. To do this, I ask the mourners to talk about the deceased and, with their permission, I take notes to base the reflections on. Talking about the life and one's memories of the deceased person can be of great therapeutic value as well as the beginning of the healing process for the bereaved as they assist in the creation of a meaningful service.

The minister will be asked for advice on the shape and content of the service. I try to make sure that the service is not a monologue from the minister and I encourage others to take part by reading, offering prayers, singing a song, playing an instrument or choosing the music and readings the deceased would have chosen. We discuss the mechanics of the service – whether there should be flowers or donations, whether it is a burial or a cremation. It is essential to ascertain whether the coffin is to be committed and family preference must be sought *before* the actual service. Psychologically, though perhaps more painful, it is thought better for the coffin to be committed. There will also need to be discussion about the possibility of a celebratory memorial service later, especially for those unable to attend the funeral.

In preparing the address or eulogy the minister needs to know the basic facts about the deceased. These will include the name the person is known by, their date of birth and date of death, details of family, whether biological or of choice, and details of the person's life. This is most important, especially if the minister has not known the deceased person. Then one must look to the partner, family members and close friends for information, through a series of meetings prior to the funeral.

Quietly, and in the bereaved person's own time, I elicit as many facts as possible, including humorous stories, foibles, sources of pride, personality traits and values, and a chronology of the deceased's life, including aspects of their early life, education, occupation, achievements and awards, recreational and community activities, faith or non-faith, life-values, and details of the family and extended family. It is essential to ascertain how much, if anything, should be said about the cause of death.

It is important to accept the fact that these meetings are not for one-to-one counselling. They are for the purpose of designing the service, including the homily, or what I call 'The Reflections', which I feel is a more correct term, especially if I have never met or known the deceased.

The reflections are not the place for theological exposition. 'Wrath of God' statements are never appropriate. It is an opportunity for guiding the mourners gently towards a healthy resolution of their grief and bereavement. If I have not known the deceased, I say so, as a prelude to offering the reflections. Occasionally the reflections may be replaced by scripted or non-scripted tributes by those wishing to give them, usually lasting between 3 and 5 minutes each. The memorial service will be of a different character, one of celebration and thanksgiving.

It is important that the funeral service, including the reflections, should be relevant to the mode of death. Even the still-born has had some life within the mother's womb. Whatever the reason for or mode of death we should be non-judgemental. We are there to try to find a meaning while at the same time being aware of the fact that we have no real answer to the 'why' questions of the bereaved. We are there to be with them, through our silence and empathy. We should be unafraid of sharing our own emotions.

As with the service, the committal will vary according to people's wishes. I was told of a funeral service where, at the graveside, bunches of daffodils were thrown on top of the coffin, after which the mourners linked arms and sang the favourite hymn of the deceased, 'Lord of the Dance', followed by each mourner taking turns to shovel in the earth, then going on to a lively wake.

In her book *Funerals to Celebrate*, Marion Barnes writes of different tributes she has witnessed and how affirmative they are of life and death. In one instance she writes about a woman who had loved nothing more than a drink and a game of cards with the neighbours:

> She had said to her family, 'When I die, I don't want you beggars standing around with long faces, and a vicar in a long dress going on about the next world. You just dig a hole, put me in, and throw in a pack of cards after me, and I'll be happy.' So, the family literally did this. After the words of committal, and the lowering of the coffin, the eldest family member broke open a brand new pack of cards, and solemnly passed one card to each person present. One by one, they approached and fluttered their card down into the grave. It was entirely relevant, and indeed reverent, being carried out with dignity and love, even if the woman's original request may have been somewhat tongue-in-cheek.[2]

Another story worth relating is of a man who had been actively involved in the catering industry. He wished his friends to toast him with a glass of champagne and this request was joyfully honoured at his cremation service. After the words of committal, the mourners were invited to surround the bier. Chilled champagne and glasses were wheeled in on a serving trolley, corks popped, glasses filled and passed around, and everyone drank a toast to the man's life as the coffin was lowered.

I was given this third example of an unusual liturgy which was very appropriate for the person who had died:

> Something had happened in Bojan's brain the day we had arranged to finalise his funeral arrangements and he was unable to speak or move. We knew most of his wishes, the church and who was to preside, that he wanted a cardboard coffin and didn't want a hearse, that he wanted a spiritual and uplifting ceremony without mention of God or Jesus, lots of his favourite music and champagne. God and Jesus had been spoiled for him by his Roman Catholic upbringing, but he firmly believed that, at the centre of everything that is meaningful, is love. We received Bojan into the church at 4 p.m. He was placed in the sanctuary and during the next eight hours his partner and friends made him and themselves at home. Tony lovingly and skilfully draped the grey cardboard coffin in yellow silk and friends arranged framed photos and albums on the altar and the credence tables along with other small possessions. We had wine and sandwiches, chatted, laughed and cried. At the service the following morning I suggested that we greet each other and people hugged, kissed and shook hands. There were no hymns or prayers but some very touching reminiscences and lots of music and, to end, a blessing using the image of divine light and love. As Bojan was taken from the church the first cork popped. Only three of us went to the crematorium. We were silent for a few moments and then signalled for the coffin to descend.

At the crematorium there is nothing to stop people sprinkling flower petals or flower heads on the coffin in the chapel, which can have a similar effect to doing this at the graveside. The most appropriate time for this to take place is during the final piece of music and before the signal is given for the coffin to move away. The principal mourners should be the first to make their offering. There is no reason why one of them should not press the release button as the committal words are spoken. I often stand at the side of the coffin while saying the committal words. I see no reason also why all present should not say the committal words with the celebrant. This may mean that the service will need to be longer than the prescribed time allotted for the service by the crematorium. If it is anticipated that the service will last longer than 20 minutes, a double booking should be arranged and confirmed with the funeral director and the crematorium manager.

The provision of a service programme is appreciated by most people. It is often used subsequently as a guide for designing one's own or another's funeral. It is increasingly common for the front of the service programme to bear a photograph of the deceased, chosen by the person themselves or the partner or a family member. Sometimes on the front of the service programme I include a single theme-like sentence, e.g. 'His life was friendship centred', or a short verse, such as the following by David Burrows:

> We must not weep at an end
> for there is no end.
> We are not what we were.
> We cannot lose what we have gained.
> We have met, we have touched each other with smiles,
> Exchanged unknown emotions.
> We have embraced without shame.
> We have met for a season,
> A brief interlude in time
> And so we part, the purpose done . . .[3]

At the wake a special memorial book may be available (with pen and coloured pencils) for people to jot down comments and reflections evoked by memories of the deceased person's life.

Today we are being increasingly caught up in the world of technology, to such an extent that we are in danger of losing our awareness that we and nature are one, all part of the whole of creation, visible and invisible. We are inseparably linked to each other – body, mind and soul, as in life so in death. We are all increasingly caught up in the profit-making society and this affects, among other things, the mechanics of the funeral and the limiting of the traditional service to 20 or 25 minutes.

However, I feel encouraged by the emergence of the green funeral service, which seems to be ecologically and spiritually sound in that it completes the eternal cycle – birth, death, decay and life. I feel that the natural death service movement is akin to the natural childbirth movement. I suspect that the green funeral service will increasingly become the norm as we begin to accept the fact that a holistic view of the person leads to a holistic view of death.

In summary, the minister must be capable of:

- being flexible in meeting the needs of the deceased person;
- coping with a service designed by others;
- helping the parents to recognise and accept the wishes of the deceased son or daughter;
- being the link person for the partner and the partner's family whenever there is disagreement;
- coping with services that are more celebrational than solemn, more spiritual than religious.
- coping with services in which details may be changed at the last moment.
- being sensitive towards the social differences between a heterosexual and a gay person's funeral;
- recognising the value that the funeral service can have for all those involved;
- recognising that difficulties may arise between the bereaved partner, family and friends in arranging the service.

As ministers, we must be clear about who the funeral is for and also be able to recognise the most significant person in the deceased's life. We may even need to ask ourselves whether the funeral is for the deceased, the partner or the family of one or both.

Whatever the type of service, it should fulfil certain requirements. It should:

- initiate the healing energies of bereavement;
- soothe the wounds of grief;
- speak directly to the mourners;
- offer something that unites rather than separates;
- offer reflections that are a tapestry of the person's life, including both good and bad points;
- encourage the message of hope;
- state clearly that the person is dead to this life;
- recognise the new role of the surviving partner;
- unfreeze the numbness of grief.

The funeral or memorial service reminds us of our place as members of the one community of God in life, in death and in life eternal. A sensitive approach to the service eases our 'going forth' into the mystery of the beyond.

> Death is another transformation
> Through which we move, an adventure,
> To surpass all adventures,
> An opening, an incredible moment of growth,
> A graduation.[4]
> Alleluia.

12. Examples of Services

This chapter contains examples of six different funeral/memorial services. Some were created by the person before his or her death, while others were co-created by the surviving partner and friends with the assistance of the pastor.

SERVICE 1

WELCOME

Well, thank you all for coming. I hope you're here because you want to be and not because you feel you ought to be.

One final instruction, don't feel guilty about anything. If we had a row, I was probably just as much to blame as you were. If you didn't come and see me as often as you think you should – I understand; I was hopeless at that sort of thing as well, so don't worry about it. As I said before, I want your memories of me to be happy ones not tinged with guilt or sadness.

Anyway, you will now be subjected to selections from the darker reaches of my record collection. I make no apologies for any of them. I know you're supposed to have opera or something, but these are my songs, and they're what I like, so if you want to do me one last service, you can sit through them and pretend you're enjoying them.

Au revoir.

EULOGY

'Old Man's Love Song' from *Lucky Bag* by Victoria Wood

As you may know, I was always a big Victoria Wood fan, so here is my favourite. It concerns an old man's reaction to the recent death of his wife. Opera lovers may sneer, but if you ask me, there is more feeling in this song than in the whole of Tosca and Carmen combined. I couldn't play this for ages after Ma died, but when I did, I realised how real it actually is. Enjoy and wallow.

Reading from *Six of One* by Rita Mae Brown

I always admired Rita Mae Brown. She manages to draw characters who fit in with everyone else regardless of their sexuality. Hers is in many ways an ideal world, where the good end happily and the bad unhappily. She also does beautiful death scenes, of which this is one. Incidentally, for those of you who like a little gossip, Rita used to go out with Martina Navratilova, and then got her own back after being dumped by taking up with Martina's ex, Judy Nelson.

'Shiver me Timbers' by Bette Midler

As Bette says, 'I've always loved songs about the sea'. The more New Age amongst you may ascribe this to my being a Pisces, but this particular song has other levels of meaning as well. I like the idea of sailing away, leaving everything behind and going to someplace better, even though you're not sure where it is, or even if it exists. You never knew I was a pioneer, did you?

Reading from *Twelfth Night* by Shakespeare (Act 1 Scene 5)

All right, I had to include a bit of culture, and this is it. *Twelfth Night* was my first brush with Shakespeare, and even formed the basis for my third year project in my drama degree. Incidentally, I inscribed this in full on the card for my grandfather's funeral, so there is also an element of continuity there as well.

'Dream a Little Dream of Me' by Cass Elliot (Mama Cass)

I always had a soft spot for Cass Elliot, a troubled soul if ever there was one. The song speaks for itself, and this is what I'd like you to do, once in a while. Incidentally, gossip-hounds, the story about her choking to death on a ham sandwich has proved false; she actually died of heart failure.

'I will follow Him' from the original soundtrack of *Sister Act*

Not a sign of last-minute religious conversion, but a great song. I think you'll like the last bit.

CLOSING PRAYERS

SERVICE 2

Entrance Music: Vangelis '1942'

INTRODUCTION AND PRAYERS

Hymn: Morning Has Broken

Morning has broken, like the first morning,
Blackbird has spoken, like the first bird.
Praise for the singing! Praise for the morning,
Praise for them, springing fresh from the Word!

Sweet the rain's new fall, sunlit from heaven,
Like the first dewfall on the first grass,
Praise for the sweetness of the wet garden,
Sprung in completeness where his feet pass.

Mine is the sunlight! Mine is the morning,
Born of the one light, Eden saw play!
Praise with elation, Praise every morning,
God's re-creation of the new day.

(ELEANOR FARJEON)

Reading: extract from *The Prophet* by Kahlil Gibran

And a youth said, speak to us of friendship. And he answered, saying:
Your friend is your needs answered. He is your field which you sow
with love and reap with thanksgiving. And he is your board and your
fireside. For you come to him with your hunger, and you seek him for
peace.

When your friend speaks his mind you fear not the 'nay' in your
own mind, nor do you with-hold the 'yay'. And when he is silent
your heart ceases not to listen to his heart; for without words, in
friendship, all thoughts, all desires, all expectations are born and shared,
with joy that is unacclaimed.

When you part from your friend, you grieve not; for that which you
loved most in him may be clearer in his absence, as the mountain to
the climber is clearer from the plain.

REFLECTIONS OF THE PERSON'S LIFE

Music: Barbra Streisand, 'Prince of Tides' Extracts

Reading: 'Distance never Separates'
Distance never separates,
Two hearts that really care.
For our memories span the miles
and in seconds, we are there.
We see the warm, familiar smile,
and deep inside we know.
That friends remain a part of us
Wherever we may go.
So we can visit anytime, no matter when or where.
For distance never separates
Two hearts that really care.
(ORIGIN UNKNOWN)

Reading: 'Death is Nothing at All' by Henry Scott Holland
Death is nothing at all. I have only slipped away into the next room.
I am I and you are you. Whatever we were to each other that we still
are. Call me by my own familiar name; speak to me in the easy way
which you always used. Put no difference in your tone, wear no false
air of solemnity or sorrow. Laugh as we always laughed at the little
jokes we enjoyed together.

Play, smile, think of me, pray for me. Let my name be the household
word that it always was. Let it be spoken without effort. Without the
ghost of a shadow on it. Life means all that it ever meant. It is the same
as it ever was; there is unbroken continuity. Why should I be out of
mind because I am out of sight? I am waiting for you, for an interval,
somewhere very near, just around the corner. All is well.

Love Changes Everything (Song from *Aspects of Love*)
Love, love changes everything,
Hands and faces, earth and sky
Love, love changes everything
How you live and how you die,
Love can make the summer fly,
Or a night seem like a life time,
Yes love, love changes everything,

Now I tremble, at your name,
Nothing in the world will ever be the same.

Love, love changes everything,
Days are longer, words mean more
Love, love changes everything,
Pain is deeper than before,
Love will turn your world around
And that world will last forever,
Yes love, love changes everything
Brings you glory, brings you shame,
Nothing in the world will ever be the same again.

Off into the world we go,
Planning futures, shaping years,
Love, but sin and suddenly,
all our wisdom disappears,
Love makes fools of everyone,
All the rules we make are broken,
Yes love, love changes everyone,
Live or perish in its flame
Love will never let you be the same.

(CLIMIE FISHER)

PRAYER AND COMMITTAL SERVICE

Music: Vivaldi, 'The Four Seasons': Spring (Concerto No. 1)

Reading: 'The Glory of Life is Love'

The Glory of Life is not that it endures forever, but that, for a time, it includes so much that is beautiful. It is a tree to those that grasp it, and happy are all who retain it. Its ways are ways of Pleasantness, and all its Paths are Peaceful. We do not demand that the flower shall never die, nor that the song shall never end. Nor would we be angry with life because one day its beauty will be dust, its music silent, and all its laughter and tears forgotten. Life, the reality, is ours; we would shape it as nobly as we can. We will not linger, like timid sailors in port, but will live dangerously, devoting ourselves with vigour to what seems to us good, beautiful and true.

The glory of Life is Love. Unending.

91

Going Forth

Song: 'Wind Beneath My Wings' by Bette Midler

LEAVING PRAYERS

Leaving song: 'The Best' by Tina Turner

'Remember the Good Times'

A Final Thought
When I am dead
Cry for me a little.
Think of me sometimes,
But not too much.
Think of me now and again.
As I was in life,
At some moments it's pleasant to recall,
But not for long.
leave me in Peace
And I shall leave you in peace.
And while you live,
Let your thoughts be with the living.

SERVICE 3

Altar party and clergy gather at the back of the church. The service begins in darkness. Congregation stand and face the back.

DEACON: Why do you seek the living among the dead? He is not here, he is risen. Let us give thanks to our God, who has delivered us from the domain of darkness and made us partakers in the inheritance of the saints in light.

Paschal candle is lit.

PRINCIPAL CELEBRANT: The light and peace of Jesus Christ be with you all.

ALL: **And also with you**.

PRINCIPAL CELEBRANT reads the Collects.

ALL: **Blessed be God forever.**

Paschal candle leads procession to the chancel, pausing three times for all to light their candles. During this the following is sung:

Hymn 93 'Gladdening Light' (by the choir alone)

Hymn 112 'Jesus lives!' (by everyone)

Deacon places candle in holder and says:

DEACON: May the light of Christ rising in glory banish all darkness from our hearts and minds.

The Gloria (*during which candles are extinguished and church lights are put on*)

ALL: **Gloria**

PRINCIPAL CELEBRANT reads the Collects

Reading: Isaiah 11:6–9

Psalm 27

RESPONSE: The Lord is my light and my salvation.

Reading: Poem based on 1 Corinthians 13

Hymn 239 'Lord of all hopefulness'

DEACON: Gospel: John 14:1–6

THE ADDRESS

Silence

THE INTERCESSIONS

PRINCIPAL CELEBRANT says the Peace

ALL: And also with you.

DEACON: Let us offer one another a sign of the Lord's peace.

Hymn 161 'Lift High the Cross' (omitting the starred verses), during which there will be a collection for HIV/AIDS research.

PRAYERS OVER THE GIFTS

The Eucharist Prayer (3)

Communion   Two anthems will be sung.

Hymn 294 'Just as I am'

Post Communion Collect

PRINCIPAL CELEBRANT: Lord of the light,
you deliver us from the power of darkness
and bring us to new life in your son;
We remember with thanksgiving your
servant —
and in this Eucharist pray that
as death recalls us to life
so by the continual presence of Jesus within
us
we may journey towards that community of
friendship

in which he now lives
and prays for us with saints of light.

ALL: **Amen**

The Anointing
—— kneels at the chancel step. Ministers gather. Principal Celebrant calls congregation to prayer.

Collect before anointing

PRINCIPAL CELEBRANT: God our healer,
who in Jesus has called us to wholeness
by our living and in our dying
anoint your servant —— by the grace of your spirit
the spirit of love and gentleness,
the spirit of strength and compassion,
the spirit of life and of courage to face life.
May we know the power of your friendship
and find your love within the community of friends
you have gathered and named your church.
Through Jesus Christ our Lord.

ALL: **Amen**

1ST MINISTER: We lay our hands upon you
in the name of Jesus Christ,
healer and lover of the world.

(Silent Prayer)

2ND MINISTER: As we anoint you outwardly with the sign of the cross,
So may the Lord of love who is more powerful
than those who would harm you,
anoint you inwardly, give you healing for all that is past
and peace for all that is to come
Lift your face to the Light
for the mark of Christ is upon you

the mark of a friend who walks with you into a new
day.

3RD MINISTER: God of love,
as our hands touch
so may our lives touch
that we may become bearers of your healing
touch,
now and always.

ALL: Amen

—— returns to his seat, ministers to their places.

PRINCIPAL CELEBRANT: The Lord be with you.

ALL: And also with you

PRINCIPAL CELEBRANT: God of tender compassion and mercy
whose son is the Morning star
and the Sun of Righteousness;
shine in the darkness
and shadows of this world,
that we may serve you in freedom and
peace,
and may the blessing of God
who calls us through healing into his light
and new life.

ALL: Amen

DEACON: Go in peace to love and serve the Lord.

ALL: In the name of Christ. Amen.

Hymn 120 'Thine Be the Glory'

SERVICE 4
WELCOME

'Why?' – Annie Lennox

'Is that love?' – Squeeze

'Everybody Hurts' – REM

'Free Man in Paris' – Joni Mitchell

THE COMMITTAL SERVICE

After the committal service:

'Let's Speak The Same Language' – Gloria Estefan

'Blue Cafe' – The Style Council

SERVICE 5

SERVICE OF THANKSGIVING

Poem: 'Love is the meaning' by David Burrows

Entrance Music: Missa Solemnis (Ind. Op. 1, 2, 3), Beethoven

OPENING PRAYERS

Hymn: 'The Lord's My Shepherd' (Crimond)

Reading: 'What is Death?' from *The Prophet* by Kahlil Gibran

Hymn: 'Morning Has Broken', N.E.H. 237

REFLECTIONS ON THE PERSON'S LIFE

Period of silence for our personal thoughts

Music: 'Ave Maria', Schubert

The Lord's Prayer

COMMITTAL SERVICE

Period of silence for our personal thoughts.

Music: 'Ave Maria', Schubert*

Please stand

We are now entrusting —— to God's unending care. We commit his body to be cremated – ashes to ashes, dust to dust, in the sure and certain hope of his journeying onwards into the greater Glory of Love, as he flows into his New Life.

Heavenly Father in your Son Jesus Christ
you have given us a true faith and a sure hope.
Strengthen this hope and this faith in us all our days,
that we may live as those who believe in

98

the communion of saints, the forgiveness of sins,
and the resurrection to eternal life;
through your Son Jesus Christ our Lord. Amen.

During the playing of the Contakion the mourners, led by the person's family and friends or his partner, will place a red rose on his coffin and leave the chapel.

Music: Russian Contakion of the Departed, N.E.H. 526

Give rest, O Christ, to thy servant with thy Saints; where sorrow and pain are no more; neither sighing, but Life everlasting. Thou art immortal, the Creator and Maker of man; and we are mortal, formed of the earth, and unto earth shall we return, for so thou didst ordain, when thou created me, saying, Dust thou art, and to dust shalt thou return. All we go down to the dust; and, weeping o'er the grave, we make our song: alleluya, alleluya, alleluya.

Give rest, O Christ, to thy servant with thy saints, where sorrow and pain are no more; neither sighing, but life everlasting.

FINAL PRAYER

May we leave this service with the assurance that love is never changed by death and that nothing of love is ever lost through death and that in the end is the harvest of a new beginning.

* The music 'Ave Maria' is included twice to provide a link where the service takes place in both a church and a crematorium.

SERVICE 6

AN ECUMENICAL SERVICE OF HOPE AND REMEMBRANCE TO MARK WORLD AIDS DAY 1995

WELCOME

The Invitation

Shared Prayer: Lord, as we worship today, give us vision.
Move us by your Spirit.
Bring good news to us all:
Freedom to broken people;
And Heaven, here on Earth.

ALL: **Open our eyes to see you as you really are and open our hearts to praise you.**

Give us a vision that will carry us through
our disappointments and our failures,
our anxious and unhappy times,
and the monotony of boring routines.

ALL: **Give us a vision that will lift our lives and lead us to new ways of service.**

Help us to dare to dream of love
in a world that speaks of hate.

ALL: **Help us to dare to dream of hope in a world that speaks of despair.**

Help us to dare to dream of peace
in a world that speaks of war.

ALL: **Help our worship today, Lord. Give us vision inspired by your spirit.**
(Copyright: Methodist Association of Youth Clubs, London Weekend)

Hymn: 'Guide me, O thou great Redeemer', N.E.H. 368

Readings: Joel 2:28–29; Romans 8:18–23

Reading: 'He wishes for the Cloths of Heaven', W. B. Yeats

Psalm: On Eagle's Wings

REFLECTIONS – based on World AIDS Day theme

Quality of life is like a wheel with many spokes, all of which contribute to its smooth running. All the spokes need to be well maintained and well tuned. If any one spoke breaks down, the rest of the wheel is affected.

We come together from many different communities but we share the need to ensure that all rights are respected and all responsibilities fulfilled.

All of us, whatever our HIV status, have the right to be treated with respect and dignity, the right to non-judgemental medical and home care and to confidentiality and non-discrimination. This includes the right of positive people to voice opinions and to be listened to, the right to be happy, sad, frightened, hopeful, angry, resigned, stubborn, joyful or any or all of these – the right to embrace life.

All of us, whatever our HIV status, have the responsibility to look after ourselves, to inform ourselves and others accurately about the risks of HIV and the realities, good and bad, about living with the virus. We share the responsibility to understand how our economy affects the lives of those with HIV and AIDS in other parts of the world, and to work with, or if necessary, against governments and international organisations wherever injustice is seen to be done.

We recognise the difficulties which these rights and responsibilities require of us. We need to be gentle with each other, and to encourage and support each other to face these challenges.

Tonight we bring these thoughts before God who loves us 'where we are', not where we or others think we should be. A God who is a God of Justice – Justice for all.

Let us remember the words of the prophet Micah: What does the Lord require of you but to do justice, and to love tenderly and to walk humbly with your God.

HYMN: 'Healer of our every ill'

PRAYERS OF INTERCESSION

Going Forth

BLESSING

DISMISSAL

Hymn: 'He who would valiant be'

PART TWO: Anthology

1. QUOTATIONS

Life – a Dying
All of life is itself a dying. My existence today is built upon the death of my yesterday; and my today will perish so that my tomorrow may come.

Norman Pittinger

The Unfinisheds
We cannot judge a biography by its length, by the number of pages in it; we must judge by the richness of the contents ... Sometimes the 'unfinisheds' are among the most beautiful symphonies.

Victor Frankl

Eternal Spring
Winter is on my head but eternal spring is in my heart. The nearer I approach the end, the plainer I hear around me the immortal symphonies of the world to come. For half a century I have been writing my thoughts in prose and verse; but I feel that I have not said one-thousandth part of what is in me. When I have gone down to the grave I shall have ended my day's work; but another day will begin the next morning. Life closes in the twilight but opens with the dawn.

Victor Hugo

One of the most important feelings to have is a satisfaction with life. Those who appreciate the value their life has to themselves and to others, enjoy life more. Recognizing that your life has meaning and that you make a difference can help lessen your anxiety about death.

Lon G. Nungesser

When you accept that you're going to die, you kid yourself a little less. Priorities change; you look at life differently. When you begin to reflect on death, you begin to live. It is part of the process of growing up.

Allegra Taylor

When you die and go to heaven our Maker is not going to ask, 'Why didn't you discover the cure for such and such? Why didn't you become the Messiah?' The only question we will be asked in that precious moment is 'Why didn't you become you?'

Elie Wiesel

Do not seek death. Death will find you. But seek the road which makes death a fulfilment.

Dag Hammarskjöld

All goes onward and outward,

Nothing collapses
And to die is different from
What anyone supposes
And luckier.

Walt Whitman

I have seen death too often to
   believe in death.
   It is not an ending, but a
   withdrawal.
As one who finishes a long
   journey
   Stills the motor, turns off the
   lights,
Steps from his car
   And walks up the path to the
   home that awaits him.

An American poet

When Rabbi Bunam was lying on
his deathbed, he said to his wife
who wept bitterly: 'Why do you
weep? All my life has been given
to me merely that I might learn
to die.'

Chasidic

In a dream we live seventy years
and discover, on awakening, that
it was a quarter of an hour. In our
life which passes as a dream, we
live seventy years, and then we
waken to a greater understanding
which shows us that it was a
quarter of an hour. Perfect understanding is beyond time.

Chasidic

One wears his mind out in study,
and yet has more mind with which
to study. One gives away his heart
in love, and yet has more heart to
give away. One perishes out of pity
for a suffering world, and is the
stronger therefor. So, too, it is
possible at one and the same time
to hold on to life and let it go. . . .

Milton Steinberg

When we are dead, and people
weep for us and grieve, let it be
because we touched their lives
with beauty and simplicity. Let it
not be said that life was good to
us, but, rather, that we were good
to life.

Jacob P. Rudin

What do our rabbis teach us about
death? We know nothing of what
is beyond the grave, and surely,
the rabbis were strict about those
who wanted to know what no man
is given to know. But they taught
us to pray: Blessed art Thou, O
Lord, who art a true friend to
those who sleep in the dust. The
rabbis taught us to pray: Blessed
art Thou, O Lord, who quickenest
the dead. We do not die into the
grave, we die into the eternity of
God.

Ignaz Maybaum

Death is the final stage of growth
in this life. There is no total death.
Only the body dies. The self or
spirit, or whatever you may wish
to label it, is eternal. You may

interpret this in any way that makes you comfortable.

Elizabeth Kübler-Ross

It is also clear that the farther one travels on the journey of life, the more births one will experience, and therefore the more deaths – the more joy and the more pain.

M. Scott Peck

In the last analysis it is our conception of death which decides the answers to all the questions that life puts to us.

Dag Hammarskjöld, DIARIES

If even dying is to be made a social function, then, please, grant me the favour of sneaking out on tip-toe without disturbing the party.

Dag Hammarskjöld, MARKINGS

There was a time when we were not. This gives us no concern – why then should it trouble us that a time will come when we shall cease to be?

William Hazlitt, TABLE TALK, 'The Fear of Death'

To die is to go into the Collective Unconscious, to lose oneself in order to be transformed into form, pure form.

Hermann Hesse, quoted in Miguel Serrano, C. G. JUNG and HERMANN HESSE

Death is but crossing the world, as friends do the sea; they live in one another still.

William Penn, SOME FRUITS OF SOLITUDE

A good death does honour to a whole life.

Petrarch, 'To Laura in Death'

The people who pretend that dying is rather like strolling into the next room always leave me unconvinced. Death, like birth, must be a tremendous event.

J. B. Priestley, OUTCRIES AND ASIDES

Death devours lambs as well as sheep.

English Proverb

To die well is the chief part of virtue.

Greek Proverb

A good death does honour to a whole life.

Italian Proverb

Death does not take the old but the ripe.

Russian Proverb

The angel of Death has many eyes.

Yiddish Proverb

Death is the side of life which is turned away from us.

Rainer Maria Rilke

2. BLESSINGS AND PRAYERS

The Lord's Prayer
Our Father in heaven. hallowed
be your name.
your kingdom come. your will be
done,
on earth as in heaven. Give us
today our daily bread.
Forgive us our sins as we forgive
those who sin against us.
Lead us not into temptation but
deliver us from evil.
For the kingdom, the power, and
the glory are yours.
Now and forever. Amen

Lord, make us an instrument of
your peace.
where there is hatred let us sow
love;
where there is injury, pardon;
where there is doubt, faith;
where there is despair, hope;
where there is darkness, light;
and where there is sadness, joy.
O Divine Master, grant that
We may not so much seek
to be consoled as to console;
To be understood as to
understand;
to be loved as to love;
for it is in giving that we receive.
it is in pardoning that we are
pardoned,
and it is in dying that we are born
to eternal life.

Prayer attributed to St Francis

Help us to accept the challenge
of AIDS:
To protect the healthy, calm the
fearful;
to offer courage to those in pain;
to embrace the dying as they flow
into love's unendingness; to
console the bereaved.
to support all those who attempt
to care for the sick and the
dying.

Enable us to offer our energies,
our imaginations
and our trusting in the mysteries
of love.
to be united with and through
one another
in liberating each other from fear
of this disease.

We offer these thoughts and
prayers in the mystery of the
loving that can and does bear
all our woundings
whatever their source through the
spirit of love's concern
for each and every person.
Amen.

Bill Kirkpatrick

An example of personalised prayer used at a funeral
Father/Mother of all creation we
give thanks for the life and love of
......, Lover, Son, Brother, Uncle,
Friend.

We remember his courage, his witnessing to the co-creative potential of his long illness. We remember his integrity of purpose. We remember his ongoing cheerfulness and sharpness of mind, his ready wit, his openness to truth, his ability to embrace us with his goodness, his humility and his friendship of love. Love that embraces and is harvested through all our life.

Father/Mother of us all, embrace us with your love, as we embrace each other's uniqueness of pain. The pain of love harvesting the all of ......'s life in ours. In this harvesting we and many others have all been touched and enriched by the mystery of ......'s loving. Embrace of his mother and father, his brothers and sisters, family and friends, ~~especially ......~~ ~~his family at ......, his family of~~ ~~volunteers~~ and his family of so many others, all knit together through the mystery of love shared, fully and freely without condition.

Father/Mother of us all, help us to emerge enriched from the depths of our grief, to see as .... did that life is for living, for loving and being loved. Help us to see as .... did that life is for sharing of pain and of joy, of death and of new life. Help us to see ......'s life as a gift and a growing and a loving left with us which cannot

ever be destroyed. He continues to live in us and we in him.

Bill Kirkpatrick

Closing Prayer ✓
Creator of us all.
we ask you to strengthen
us this hour, this day
with the courage of faith,
with the hope of love.
as together we release ....
As he flows into the undying
mystery of love.
Within the river of life flowing
between this dimension
and the next. Nurtured
by The Love that contains
all understanding.

Bill Kirkpatrick

Heavenly Father in your Son
Jesus Christ
you have given us a true faith and
a sure hope.
Strengthen this hope and this
faith in us all our days.
that we may live as those who
believe in
the communion of saints, the
forgiveness of sins,
and the resurrection to eternal
life;
through your Son Jesus Christ
our Lord. Amen.

Bill Kirkpatrick

Creator, Lover of us all, we give
back to you ...... who you gave to
us. As you did not lose .... when
you gave him to us, so we do not

109

lose ...... by returning him to you.
Your dear son taught us that life
is eternal and that love cannot die.
So death is only a horizon, and a
horizon is only the limit of our
sight. Open our eyes to see more
clearly, and draw us closer to you
that we may know that we are
nearer to our loved ones, who
are eternally in the embracing of
your loving care. You have told us
that you are preparing a place for
us: prepare us also for that place
in the beyond of this life. Help us
to know and feel that love is never
changed by death and that
nothing of love is ever lost
through death and that in the end
is the harvest of a new beginning.

Bill Kirkpatrick (adapted)

Father, Mother of us all
it is through your loving
you have offered us
the courage of faith
and the hope of love.
Strengthen these gifts
in us today and always.
Enabling us to live and be
as persons who believe
in the community of
the Friendships of love,
Amen

Bill Kirkpatrick (adapted)

Day by day, day by day
Dear Lord, three things I pray:
To see thee more clearly,
Love thee more dearly
Follow thee more nearly,

Day by day, day by day.

St Richard of Chichester

May the Lord support us all the
day long,
till the shades lengthen and the
evening comes.
and the busy world is hushed.
and the fever of life is over,
and our work is done.
Then in his mercy
may he give us a safe lodging,
and a holy rest,
and peace at the last. Amen

John Henry Newman

The Blessing

Time there was – but it is gone
Time there may be – who can
tell?
Time there is to act upon,
Help us, Lord, to use it well.

Anon.

Prayer for Those Dying of AIDS

O God of love, whose mercy has
always included those whom we
have forgotten, those whom we
have isolated, and those who
suffer, bless we beseech you all
who are afflicted with HIV/
AIDS. Comfort them in their
pain, sustain them in their days
of hopelessness, and receive them
into the arms of your mercy in
their dying. Open our hearts to
provide for their needs, to take
away their isolation, to share their
journey of suffering and sorrow,

and to be present with them that no one need die alone. Bless those who mourn the death of their friends and lovers that they may not be overwhelmed by death but may receive comfort and strength to meet the days ahead with trust and hope in your goodness and mercy: in Jesus' name we pray. Amen.

Prayer for Persons with AIDS

Hear our prayer, O God of mercy and love,
for all who suffer with AIDS.
Grant unto them tender and loving companions
who will support them in the midst of fear,
Give them hope for each day to come
that every day may be lived with courage and faith.
Bless them with an abundance of your love
that they may live with concern for others
and not be obsessed with own illness.
Pour upon them the peace and wholeness
which you alone can give;
through Jesus Christ, our Saviour,
who came to give us abundant life,
we pray. Amen.

Vienna Cobb Anderson

Thanksgiving for a Life

We thank you, O God,
for the life of ....
for the love that he shared so abundantly,
for the warmth of his laughter,
for the joy of his presence,
for the easy conversation we knew,
for his clear articulation of thought and feeling,
for his openness and direct way,
for his compassion for others
for the spontaneity of his heart,
for the generosity of his soul,
for the companionship he gave,
for the years we spent together.
for his friendship and love.
for the wondrous beauty of his life.
For these and all the blessings
that .... gave to us,
we thank you, O God of love.
Amen.

Vienna Cobb Anderson

We are here, each one of us
To thank God
For the life of ....
For the love .... shared so fully
For the warmth of .... laughter
For the joy of .... presence
For the easy conversation ....
shared
For .... articulation of thought and feeling
For .... readiness to hear through listening
For .... empathy of compassion for others

For .... generosity, so often
   hidden
For the companionship ....
   gave
For .... aliveness to all life
For .... friendship of concern
For these and all the blessings
That .... gave to each one of us
We thank you .... as we thank
Our God of love for your
continuing presence in our lives.

        We thank you, O God
   (Adapted from Vienna Cobb Anderson)
   (Insert his/her where appropriate.)

Anointing

Blessing of the oil
Eternal and loving God.
bless this oil
and bless those who receive its
   anointing in trust.
that it may be to them
an eternal medicine.
a spiritual remedy.
an inward consecration.
to their strengthening, healing,
   and joy:
through Jesus Christ our Saviour.

Bidding to all
In the name of God.
giving life, bearing pain, making
   whole:
by this oil
may we/you be warmed and
   soothed:
may the healing Spirit
that we/you may become whole,
penetrate the cells and fibres of
   our/your being,

giving thanks to God always and
   in all places,
and being ready to venture on the
   way of faith:
by this oil
may we/you renew the
   consecration of our/your life
to the truth and service of God
being not afraid to encounter
   God alone,
nor of dying in order to live,
nor of bearing the burdens of
   others
with whom we/you have to do;
know this oil
as a sign of gladness and rejoicing,
of lamps lit and of feasting.
of mirth and of joy.

To each who receives anointing
.... through faith in the power
   and the will
of our Saviour Jesus Christ
to make you whole and holy, to
   consecrate you with joy
for ever deeper service and
   friendship
to give you courage
to go through the narrow gates of
   your journey,
I anoint you with oil
in the name of God
who gives you life,
bears your pain
and makes you whole.
Amen.

        Jim Cotter

Prayer on the Anniversary of the Death of Life Partner

Lord God, Lord of Life and
Death,
today, I recall the death of my
beloved.
My heart still bears the stain of
tears
from that great day of loss.
Our lives had so become one
that a part of me died
when (name) .... died.
Like two rivers that had joined as
one,
our two lives flowed together
in joyful communion and
affection.
You, Lord and God.
were the one who arranged our
union,
and You, Divine Mystery of
Love,
were the fire of love between us.
I recall today, in prayer,
how he/she changed my life
and called forth from me all that
was good and holy,
Like a mirror, I saw myself
reflected in him/her
and so was able to face my
failings and shortcomings
in my struggle to be worthy of
Your gift of love.

As I recall and relive that day of
sorrow,
I rejoice and am grateful
for the great treasure of memories
that I possess.
Those years together are alive

and continue to nourish me with
life.
I firmly believe that (name) ....
has not ceased to exist but is alive,
fully alive and happy within Your
sacred embrace.
I firmly believe and know
that love is beyond the touch of
death
and that our love for each other
remains
and awaits our final union
together with You.

I seek. Lord, a favor from You:
when the time comes for me to
open the door of death
and journey to You.
grant that (name) .... may
come and take my hand,
guiding me along the dark and
mysterious way
which leads to the wedding feast
of eternity.
Lord of Compassion.
be with me as I await that day
and grant eternal joy and peace
to my beloved
and to all the holy dead.
Amen.

Edward Hays

Prayer on the anniversary of the death of a friend

Lord of Life and Death,
today, I remember the death of
(name) ....
whose life touched mine
and added to the richness of my
existence.

I pause to recall the good times
    that we shared together.
(Pause for silent reflection.)

I am grateful that these are
    imperishable treasures
which I will carry with me into
    eternity.
Within the mystery of Your
    divine plan,
our life-pathways came together
and blended as parallel pathways.
I am grateful today
for all that we shared in our times
    together,
for humor and work, for affection
    and trust,
for the celebration of life.

Lord of compassion,
we are all sinners and in need of
    divine healing,
so grant to (name) whatever is
    needed
so that he/she can rejoice forever
in Your divine friendship and
    eternal care.
Gracious Lord,
I lift up into Your Divine Heart,
    my friend
and ask that you grant to him/
    her eternal peace
and the perpetual company of
    your saints. Amen.

Edward Hays

A Prayer

To those that I love and must
    leave behind;
Do not cry for me when these
    words you find;

When I am gone and free, just
    let me go;
I have so many things to see and
    do;
You musn't tie yourself to me with
    tears,
Be happy that we had so many
    years.

Anon.

Blessed are you, our God, for in
Jesus you show us the image of
your glory. We give thanks for the
gospel of healing and liberation
which is preached to the whole
Church in the ministry of those
with HIV or AIDS. May we
recognise that it is the real body of
Christ which suffers at this time
through HIV and AIDS. It is the
real mind of Christ which is
racked by fear and confusion. It
is the real image of God in Christ
which is blasphemed in prejudice,
oppression and poverty. May we
see in this crisis, loving God, not
punishment but the place where
God is most powerfully at work
in Jesus Christ, and where, as
sisters and brothers, we can lead
each other to life in all its fullness,
given in the same Christ our Lord.
Amen.

Catholic AIDS Link

A Benediction

May the Lord who walks beside
    you reach out and take your
    hand;

May you hear his loving voice and
feel his warmth.

May the heart which died and
lives for you beat close to yours
this day

And the soul which starves
within you now be fed.

May you see the shining glory
which he showers all around;

May his love restore the wounds
which you still bear.

May your heart which pained and
ached in you beat wildly, glad
with joy

And may you see his presence in
your life.

He is with you – may you know
it.

He loves you – may you feel it.

He suffered and he died that you
might not.

May you walk in peace and
plenty.

In safety and in love.

Till you travel the final journey
to him

Above.

Amen.

A Benediction
May the Lord, who himself suffered grief and sorrow and who
carries your griefs and sorrows,
comfort you, strengthen you,
sustain you and give you peace.
Amen.

Aztec Prayer to God
Oh, only for so short a while
have you loaned us to each other.

Because we take form in your act
of drawing us,

and we breathe in your singing us.

But only for a short while

have you loaned us to each other.

Because even a drawing cut in
crystalline obsidian fades,

and the green feathers, the crown
feathers,

of the Quetzal bird lose their
colour,

and even the sounds of the
waterfall

die out in the dry season.

So, we too, because only for a
short while

have you loaned us to each other.

A Prayer from the Taoist Tradition
We are born gentle and weak.
At death we are hard and stiff.
Green plants are tender and filled
with sap. When they die they are
withered and dry. Therefore the
stiff and unbending are the
disciples
of death. The gentle and yielding
are the disciples of life.

Lao Tzu

A Prayer adapted from the Judaic Tradition (Dt. 6:5)
You shall love the Lord your God
with all your heart, and with all
your soul and with all your mind.
And you shall love your neighbour
as yourself.

A Prayer from the Hasidic Tradition

Do not think that the words of
prayer as you say them go up to
God.
It is not the words themselves
that
ascend; rather it is the burning
desire of your heart that rises like
smoke to heaven. If your prayer
consists only of words and letters,
but does not contain your heart's
desire, how can it rise up to God?

O God, early in the morning I
cry to you.
Help me to pray
And to concentrate my thoughts
on you.
I cannot do this alone.
In me there is darkness,
But with you there is light;
I am lonely, but you do not leave
me;
I am feeble in heart, but with you
there is help;
I am restless, but with you there
is peace.
In me there is bitterness, but with
you there is patience;
I do not understand your ways,
But you know the way for me . . .
Restore me to liberty,
And enable me so to live now
That I may answer before you and
before me.
Lord, whatever this day may
bring,
Your name be praised.

Dietrich Bonhoeffer

Make speed to aid him, ye saints
of God; come forth to meet him,
ye angels of the Lord; Receiving
his soul, Presenting him before the
face of the most highest. May
Christ receive thee, who hath
called thee; and may angels bear
thee into the bosom of Abraham.
Receiving his soul; presenting him
before the face of the most
highest. Rest eternal grant unto
him, O Lord, and let light perpetual shine upon him. Presenting
him before the face of the most
highest.

Commendation of a soul, Western Rite

With the souls of the righteous
dead, give rest, O Saviour, to the
soul of thy servant N., preserving
him unto the life of blessedness
which is with thee. O thou who
lovest mankind.

In the place of thy rest, where all
thy saints repose, give rest also to
the soul of thy servant N., for thou
alone lovest mankind.
Glory be to the Father . . .
Thou are the God who didst
descend into hell and loose the
bonds of the captives. Do thou
give rest also to the soul of thy
servant N.
Both now and for ever . . .

O Virgin, alone pure and unde-
filed, who without seed didst
bring forth God, pray thou that
his soul may be saved.
With the saints give rest, O

Christ, to the soul of thy servant N., where there is neither sickness, nor sorrow, nor sighing, but life everlasting.

Prayers for the dead, Orthodox

Blessed is the path thou goest on this day, for a place of rest is prepared for thee.

Burial of the dead, Orthodox

O Father of all, we pray to thee for those whom we love, but see no longer. Grant them thy peace; let light perpetual shine upon them; and in thy loving wisdom and almighty power work in them the good purpose of thy perfect will; through Jesus Christ our Lord.

Book of Common Prayer

The souls of the righteous are in the hand of God and there shall no torment touch them. In the sight of the unwise they seemed to die, but they are in peace. Alleluia.

Offertory, Feast of All Saints, Western Rite

I am going now into the sleep,
Be it that I in health shall wake;
If death be to me in deathly sleep,
Be it that in thine own arm's keep,
O God of grace, to new life I wake;
O be it in thy dear arm's keep
O God of grace, that I shall awake!

Poems of the Western Highlanders

O Lord God, the life of mortals, the light of the faithful, the strength of those who labour and the repose of the dead; grant us a tranquil night free from all disturbance; that after an interval of quiet sleep, we may, by thy bounty, at the return of light be endued with activity from the Holy Spirit and enabled in security to render thanks to thee.

Mozarabic

O Lord, may the end of my life be the best of it; may my closing acts be my best acts, and may the best of my days be the day when I shall meet Thee.

A closing Muslim Prayer

A version of the prayer Jesus taught his friends

Father and Mother of us all,
you are love through and through,
and we bless You.
Let your new world come,
let what you long for be always done,
in everyone, everywhere – and in us.
Be near enough to reach our need every day.
Be gentle enough to forgive us the hurt we have done to You –
as we are gentle and forgive in our turn.
Never let us fall
but draw us away from evil and the dark.

For we know the world that is
  coming is Yours,
all Yours, in richness and beauty
  and splendour. Amen.

The Revd Simon Bailey

Loving God, we pray in a special way today with and for all women living with HIV or AIDS. We pray that they may be freed of all pain – physical, emotional and spiritual. May we all experience your steadfast love. We give thanks for the witness of so many women, living with HIV, caring for partners and children. We praise you for their strength and vitality, even in the midst of suffering and their nurturing ministry when many of us would falter. We rejoice in the gifts of women exercised in ministry amongst all your people, particularly those who suffer. Lead us all to look upon you, O God, where all death is vanquished in a place of glory for ever and ever.
Amen.

Catholic AIDS Link

May the road rise up to meet you, may the wind be always at your back, may the sun shine warm upon your face, the rain fall soft upon your fields, and until we meet again, may God – whatever you conceive him to be – hold you in the palm of his hand.

Celtic Blessing

Prayer for Serenity

God, grant me the serenity
to accept the things I cannot
  change,
courage to change the things I
  can,
and wisdom to know the
  difference,
living one day at a time,
enjoying one moment at a time,
accepting hardship as a pathway
  to peace,
taking, as Jesus did, this sinful
  world as it is,
not as I would have it,
trusting that You will make all
  things right
if I surrender to Your will,
so that I may be reasonably happy
  in this life
and supremely happy with You
  forever in the next.

Reinhold Niebuhr

Committal Prayers

Let us commend our brother/
sister .... to the mercy of God
our Maker and Redeemer.

O God give him/her rest in the place where green things grow, that delightful garden where pain and grief and sighing are unknown. Holy Lord God, heaven and earth are full of your Holy Loving.

Go forth upon thy journey from this world, O Christian soul,
In the name of God the Father

Almighty who created thee.
Amen.
In the name of Jesus Christ who
suffered for thee. Amen.
In the name of the Holy Spirit
who strengtheneth thee. Amen.
In communion with the Blessed
Virgin Mary, Mother of God, and
the blessed Saints, and aided by
Angels and Archangels, and all
the armies of the heavenly host.
Amen.

Give rest, O Christ, to thy servant
with thy saints: where sorrow and
pain are no more: neither sighing,
but Life everlasting. Thou art
immortal, the Creator and Maker
of man: and we are mortal,
formed of the earth, and unto
earth shall we return: for so thou
didst ordain, when thou createdst
me, saying, Dust thou art, and to
dust thou shalt return. All we go
down to the dust: and weeping
o'er the grave, we make our song:
alleluya, alleluya.

To everything there is a season, a
time to every purpose on earth.
A time to be born, and a time to
die. During this last act of our
celebration of ....'s life, we are
in sorrow, but without fear, with
love and appreciation. We entrust
........'s body to God's keeping
within the safe bosom of Mother
earth, which sustains and renews
all life.

With this hope we are now
entrusting .... to God's
unending care. Together we now
commit his body to be buried,
dust to dust, and in the sure and
certain hope of his journeying ever
onwards into the greater glory of
love eternal, as he enters his new
life.

Creator of us all, strengthen us
this day, at this time, with the
courage of faith, with the hope of
love, as we release .... into the
peace, the love that contains all
understanding. Amen.

We have entrusted .... to God's
merciful keeping, and we now
commit his body to the ground (*or*
to be cremated): (earth to earth
ashes to ashes, dust to dust:) in
the sure and certain hope of the
resurrection to eternal life through
our Lord Jesus Christ, who died,
was buried, and rose again for us.
To him be glory for ever and ever.

Almighty God, Father of all
mercies and giver of all comfort:
Deal graciously, we pray, with
those who mourn, that casting all
their care on you, they may know
the consolation of love's unendingness. Amen.

Creator of all, strengthen us this
day, with the courage of faith, with
the hope of love, as together we
flow into the undying mystery of

love that is the river of life
between this life and the next as
we release our .... into peace and
the love that contains all understanding. Amen.

The Lord is full of compassion
and mercy, slow to anger and of
great goodness. As a Father is
tender towards his children, so
is the Lord tender to those who
fall short of the mark. For he
knows whereof we are made, he
remembers that we are but dust.
The days of man are but as grass:
he flourishes like a flower of the
field, when the wind goes over it,
it is gone, and its place will
know it no more. But the merciful
goodness of the Lord endures for
ever and ever.

Final Prayers

God of all mystery, whose ways
are beyond understanding,
lead us, who grieve at this
   untimely death,
to a new and deeper faith in your
   love
which brought your Son Jesus
the young prince of glory,
into resurrection life.

Gentle Lord,
your servant has come
by a hard and painful road
into the valley of death.
Lead him/her now into the place
where there is no more pain.

Forgiving God,
in the face of death we discover
how many things are still undone,
how much might have been done
   otherwise.
Redeem our failure.
Bind up the wounds of past
   mistakes.
Transform our guilt to active love,
and by your forgiveness make us
   whole.

Lord, you alone are the source of
   life,
may your life-giving Spirit flow
   through us.
grant us your compassion one for
   the other,
in our sorrow give us the calm of
   your peace,
kindle our hope and let our grief
   give way to joy,
through Jesus Christ our Lord.

*From the General Synod of the Scottish
Episcopal Church's Revised Funeral Rites*

O God who brought us to birth.
and in whose arms we die;
in our grief and shock
contain and comfort us;
embrace us with your love,
give us hope in our confusion,
and grace to let go into new life,
through Jesus Christ. Amen.

Janet Morley

Eternal God, sustainer of all life,
giver of all good things: Look
upon this gathering of your
people. Let love transform our

lives, that anger may give way to peace, that despair may give way to hope, that out of sorrow may come joy. May we in the midst of pain, find signs of the life which is yours.

Anon.

Bidding Prayers

Father of all Creation
We offer our thanks
For the life of ....
For his artistic gifts
For his loving friendships
For his uniqueness as a person

Mother of all Creation
We offer our thanks for ....'s family
For his friends here present
and for those around the world.
As we share the pain of bereavement.

Father of all, we offer our thanks
For all those involved
In the caring of ....
Especially the care team at ....

Father of all loving, We remember in the friendships of love,
All those who with .... have died of opportunistic infections
And who in their dying have given us so much to be proud of as they flowed into the greater mystery.

Creator of all, it is through your loving that you have offered us a true faith and a sure hope.
Strengthen this faith and this hope in us always, that we may live as those who believe in the Kingdom of Love and our mutual growth into Eternal Life.

Anon.

It is now time to take our leave of .... whom we all remember through our proud mourning, yet with a great warmth of love's friendships. For all he/she means for each one of us, embraced as we are for all time, by the uniqueness of his/her personality. We return to our daily living, to our differing friendships of love, with the resolve to follow his/her example of courage, of sharing unconditionally. To live our lives more fully and with the same purpose, cheerfulness and love. We leave this service of thanksgiving from the midst of our proud mourning, knowing that love is never changed by death, that in the end is a harvest of a new beginning.

Bill Kirkpatrick (adapted)

Blessings

The Blessing of God
Giver of Life,
Bearer of Pain,
Creator and Sustainer,

121

Liberator and Redeemer.
Healer and Sanctifier,
Be with you
And all whom you love
Both living and departed,
Now and forever. Amen.

Jim Cotter

You, O Lord, are the endless power that renews life beyond death; You are the greatness that saves. You care for the living with love. You renew life beyond death with unending mercy. You support the falling, and heal the sick. You free prisoners, and keep faith with those who sleep in the dust. Who can perform such mighty deeds, and who can compare with you, a king who brings death and life, and renews salvation. You are faithful to renew life beyond death. Blessed are You, Lord, who renews life beyond death.

Jewish Prayer

My Lord God, I have no idea where I am going. I do not see the road ahead of me. I cannot know for certain where it will end. Nor do I really know myself, and the fact that I think that I am following your will does not mean that I am actually doing so. But I believe that the desire to please you does in fact please you. And I hope I have that desire in all that I am doing. I hope that I will never do anything apart from that desire. And I know that if I do

this you will lead me by the right road though I may know nothing about it. Therefore I will trust you always, though I may seem to be lost and in the shadow of death I will not fear, for you are ever with me, and you will never leave me to face my perils alone.

Fr Louis Merton OCSO (Thomas Merton)

O God of the living in whose
   embrace all creatures live,
in whatever world or condition
   they may be,
I pray for those whom I have
   known and loved,
whose names and needs and
   dwelling place are known to
   you.
And give you thanks for my
   memories of them.
In you, O God, I love them.
May this prayer minister to their
   growing and their peace;
in and through Jesus Christ
who broke the barrier of death
and lives for evermore.

Jim Cotter

The Lord bless us and keep us.
The Lord make his face to shine
upon us and be gracious to us.
The Lord lift up his countenance
upon us and give us peace, today
and evermore. Amen

Nb. 6:24–26

Leaving Prayer
Let us go out into the world,
glad that we have loved,

free to weep for the one whom
we have lost,
free to hold each other in our
human frailty
empowered to love to the full, as
did *N*,
and to affirm the hope of human
existence.
Amen. So be it.

Anon.

O Father-Mother God, ever
loving and ever living, the final
reality in which all souls find their
completion, rest and fulfilment,
we pray for him whom you know
and love far more deeply than we
can ever imagine. Give him your
light and love for which he sought
so fervently. In your mercy heal,
strengthen, enlighten, and guide
him as he enters the unbounded
and mysterious vistas of eternity.
May his immortal being reveal
more and more the infinite
potential of wisdom, joy and compassion with which you endow the
human soul. May he know the
intimate fellowship of the children
of God and become an
ambassador of your caring and
peace to all dimensions of your
universe.

O Gracious One, let him know
how much we love and miss his
physical presence and long to be
with him. Grant that he may be
allowed to guide and guard our
journey until we meet in that condition where partings cease. Until
then give us a sense of his loving
presence. Heal all his wounds
inflicted by an insensitive and
unconscious society. Let us minister in any way we can to his
growth, peace, and joy. Let us do
nothing that keeps us from fellowship together in the communion
of saints. We ask this of you, a
loving God who created us, saw
our misery, came among us, suffered with us, suffered for us, and
by rising again opened to us the
portals of eternal life. Amen.

Morton Kelsey

The Blessing

God the healer, bless our world
infected with this disease; Jesus
the healer, bless the affected with
courage and hope; Spirit of
Healing within, bless each of us
with life ever new; here and everywhere, now and always. Amen.

The Revd Simon Bailey

3. POEMS

Not, how did he die, but how did
  he live?
Not, what did he gain, but what
  did he give?
These are the units to measure
  the worth
Of a man as a man, regardless of
  birth.
Not what was his church, nor
  what was his creed?
But had he befriended those
  really in need?
Was he ever ready, with word of
  good cheer,
To bring back a smile, to banish
  a tear?
Not what did the sketch in the
  newspaper say,
But how many were sorry when
  he passed away?

Anon.

When

When mine hour is come
Let no teardrop fall
And no darkness hover
Round me where I lie.
Let the vastness call
One who was its lover,
Let me breathe the sky.
Where the lordly light
Walks along the world,
And its silent tread
Leaves the grasses bright,
Leaves the flowers uncurled,
Let me to the dead

Breathe a gay good-night.

A. E. (George Russell)

Come into the candlelight. I'm
  not afraid
to look the dead in the face. When
  they return,
they have a right, as much as other
  Things do,
to pause and refresh themselves
  within our vision.
Come; and we will be silent for
  a while.
Look at this rose on the corner of
  my desk:
isn't the light around it just as
  timid
as the light on you? It too should
  not be here,
it should have bloomed or faded
  in the garden,
outside, never involved with me.
  But now
it lives on in its small porcelain
  vase:
what meaning does it find in my
  awareness?

Rainer Maria Rilke from REQUIEM FOR A
FRIEND *(trans. Stephen Mitchell)*

Some walk with Death as to a
  leper tied,
and some hold hands as with a
  summer bride,
and her warm presence serves to
  red the cheek:

some know her not, nor knowing,
  fear her state:
some grow too fond impatiently
  to wait,
and distraught, perfect
  consummation seek.

Jim Bailey, from DEATH IN THE AIRCREW
MESS, DEBRIEFING

When lilacs last in the dooryard
  bloom'd,
And the great star early droop'd
  in the western sky in the
  night,
I mourn'd, and yet shall mourn
  with ever-returning spring.

Ever-returning spring, trinity
  sure to me you bring,
Lilac blooming perennial and
  drooping star in the west,
And thought of him I love.

Walt Whitman

Take of me what is not my own,
my love, my beauty, and my
  poem,
the pain is mine, and mine alone.

See how against the weight in the
  bone
the hawk hangs perfect in mid-
  air –
the blood pays dear to raise it
  there,
the moment, not the bird, divine.

And see the peaceful trees extend
their myriad leaves in leisured
  dance –

they bear the weight of sky and
  cloud
upon the fountain of the veins.

In rose with petals light as air
I bind for you the tides and fire –
the death that lives within the
  flower
oh gladly, love, for you I bear.

Kathleen Raine, ENVOI

I had thought that your death
Was a waste and a destruction
A pain of grief hardly to be
  endured.
I am only beginning to learn
That your life was a gift and a
  growing
And a loving left with me,
That desperation of death
Destroyed the existence of love,
But the fact of death
Cannot destroy what has been
  given.
I am learning to look at your life
  again
Instead of your death and your
  departing.

Marjorie Pizer, THE EXISTENCE OF LOVE

Let Me Walk in Beauty
Let me walk in beauty
and make my eyes ever behold
the red and purple sunset.
Make my hands respect the
  things you have made,
and my ears sharp to hear your
  voice
Make me wise so that I may
  understand

the things you have taught my
  people.
Let me learn the lessons you have
  hidden
in every leaf and rock.
I seek strength
not to be greater than my brother
but to fight my greatest enemy:
myself.
Make me always ready to come
  to you
with clean hands and straight
  eyes.
So when life fades
as a fading sunset
my spirit may come to you
  without shame.
Thank you.

North American Indian Prayer

When You Love
When you love, give it everything
  you have got.
And when you have reached your
  limit, give it more,
and forget the pain of it.
Because as you face your death
it is only the love that you have
  given and received
which will count,
and all the rest:
the accomplishments, the
  struggle, the fights
will be forgotten in your
  reflection.
And if you have loved well
then it will all have been worth it.
And the joy of it will last you
  through the end.
But if you have not,

death will always come too soon
and be too terrible to face.

Richard Allen

I Want to Love You
I want to love you without
  clutching,
appreciate you without judging,
join you without invading,
invite you without demanding,
leave you without guilt,
evaluate you without blaming
and help you without insulting.
If I can have the same from you,
then we can truly meet and enrich
  each other.

Virginia Satir

Do not say that I'll depart
  tomorrow
because even today I still arrive

Look deeply I arrive in every
  second
to be a bud on a spring branch
to be a tiny bird, with wings still
  fragile
    learning to sing in my new
      nest,
to be a caterpillar in the heart of
  a flower,
to be a jewel Hiding itself in a
  stone

I still arrive, in order to laugh and
  to cry,
  in order to fear and to hope,
the rhythm of my heart is the
  birth and
death of all that are alive.

North American Indian

126

The day we die
the wind comes down
to take away
our footprints

The wind makes dust
to cover up
the marks we left
while walking

For otherwise
the thing would seem
as if we were
still living.

Therefore the wind
is he who comes
to blow away
our footprints.

Southern Bushmen

Dear Lovely Death

Dear lovely Death
That taketh all things under
  wing –
Never to kill –
Only to change
Into some other thing
This suffering flesh,
To make it either more or less,
But not again the same –
Dear lovely Death
Change is thy other name.

Langston Hughes

To open eyes when others close
  them
to hear when others do not wish
  to listen
to look when others turn away
to seek to understand when
  others give up

to rouse oneself when others
  accept
to continue the struggle even
  when one is not the strongest
to cry out when others keep
  silent –
to be a Jew
it is that,
it is first of all that
and further
to live when others are dead
and to remember when others
  have forgotten.

Emmanuel Eydoux (translated from the
French by Jonathan Magonet)

Life After Death

These things I know:
  How the living go on living
  and how the dead go on
    living with them
so that in a forest
  even a dead tree casts a shadow
  and the leaves fall one by one
and the branches break in the
  wind
and the bark peels off slowly
and the trunk cracks
  and the rain seeps in through
    the cracks
and the trunk falls to the ground
and the moss covers it
  and in the spring the rabbits
    find it
and build their nest
inside the dead tree
so that nothing is wasted in
  nature
  or in love.

Laura Gilpin

Let the dreams that are gone
  asleep fast my love,
  Let the tears and fears of
  yesterday's storm,
For the darkness you saw is past
  my love,
  So smile a new day is born.
The seasons of life will go on my
  love,
  And the sails of yours may be
  torn
But the secrets beneath your feet
  my love,
  Are the flowers yet to be born.
Let the tears that you shed fall
  sweet my love,
  For the pain goes and rainbows
  come without warning
All the seasons will surely return
  my love
  And a new life will be born in
  the dawning.

Author unknown, adapted by Bill
Kirkpatrick

We must not weep at an end
For there is no end.
We are not what we were.
We cannot lose what we have
  gained.
We have met, we have touched
  each other with smiles,
Exchanged unknown emotions.
We have embraced without
  shame.
We have met for a reason,
A brief interlude in time,
And so we part, the purpose
  done. . . .

David Burrows

The Reassurance

About ten days or so
After we saw you dead
You came back in a dream.
I'm all right now you said.

And it *was* you, although
You were fleshed out again:
You hugged us all round then,
And gave your welcoming beam.

How like you to be kind,
Seeking to reassure.
And, yes, how like my mind
To make itself secure.

Thom Gunn

Death is not The End

Death is not The End
But the beginning
Of a metamorphosis.
For matter is never destroyed –
  Only transformed
And rearranged –
Often more perfectly.
Witness how in the moment of
  the caterpillar's death
The beauty of the butterfly is
  born
And released from the prison of
  the cocoon
It flies free.

Peter Tatchell

For as long as space exists
And sentient beings endure,
May I too remain,
To dispel the misery of the world.

Lord make me an instrument
Of thy peace, where there is hatred,

Let me sow love;
Where there is injury, pardon;
Where there is doubt, faith;
Where there is despair, hope;
Where there is darkness, light;
And where there is sadness, joy.
O Divine Master, grant that
I may not so much seek
To be consoled as to console;
To be understood as to understand;
To be loved as to love;
For it is in giving that we receive,
It is in pardoning that we
Are pardoned, and it is in dying
That we are born to eternal life.

Sogyal Rinpoche

When to the sessions of sweet
　silent thought
I summon up remembrance of
　things past,
I sigh the lack of many a thing I
　sought,
And with old woes new wail my
　dear time's waste;
Then can I drown an eye, unused
　to flow,
For precious friends hid in death's
　dateless night,
And weep afresh love's long since
　cancelled woe,
And moan th'expense of many a
　vanished sight;
Then can I grieve at grievances
　foregone,
And heavily from woe to woe tell
　o'er
The sad account of fore-
　bemoanèd moan,

Which I new pay as if not paid
　before:
But if the while I think on thee,
　dear friend,
All losses are restored and
　sorrows end.

William Shakespeare

I wish I could translate the hints
　about the dead young men and
　women,
And the hints about old men and
　mothers, and the offspring
　taken soon out of their laps.

What do you think has become
　of the young and old men?
And what do you think has
　become of the women and
　children?

They are alive and well
　somewhere;
The smallest sprout shows there
　is really no death,
And if ever there was it led
　forward life, and does not wait
　at the end to arrest it,
And ceased the moment life
　appeared.

All goes onward and outward. . . .
　and nothing collapses,
And to die is different from what
　any one supposed, and luckier.

Walt Whitman

Silent grief
When one's friend, that special
　friend,
passes on their journey home

129

one's world is torn apart – walls
crumble –
one questions life about life
simple things seem so complex
easy tasks take on an enormous
weight . . .

It is a traumatic experience at the
best of times
but makes it ten fold when one
can't talk
to be able to share the pain one
feels
because it is a hidden grief that
one can't
tell others about – one has to
suffer in silence . . .

But one must air one's sadness to
overcome
silence only makes pain more
unbearable
your friend wouldn't want this
measure of pain – not for you!
for your friend is still by your side,
to help you,
to guide you as they have done
for a lifetime
the only difference is you can't see
them
but they walk beside you as
always . . .

So be comforted by this and as
time goes by
your own self will shine again
the one that they loved you
for . . .
remember the times that you
shared

and the warmth that the
friendship gave to both
smile within from the fond
memories that you both
cherished
and be thankful that your lives
crossed
for both were richer for it and the
world a poorer place without

B. J. Allen

Loss of a Gay or Lesbian Lover

Our thoughts turn to those who
have died; people of every race and
nation whose lives have been a
blessing, enriching our own.

O God, remember today our
gay sisters and brothers who were
martyred in years past: those who
were murdered by fanatics in the
middle ages, those who perished
in the Holocaust, and those struck
down in our own city, in our own
time. Remember also those driven
to despair by a world that hated
them because of their love for one
another, who took their own lives.
And in mercy remember those
who have wasted their lives by
suppressing their true natures and
refraining from sharing their love
with one another. O God, accept
the sacrifice of these martyrs, and
help us bring an end to hate and
oppression of every kind.

Author Unknown

Each Of Us Has a Name

Each of us has a name
given by God

and given by our parents
Each of us has a name
given by our stature and our smile
and given by what we wear
Each of us has a name
given by the mountains
and given by our walls
Each of us has a name
given by the stars
and given by our neighbors
Each of us has a name
given by our sins
and given by our longing
Each of us has a name
given by our enemies
and given by our love
Each of us has a name
given by our celebrations
and given by our work
Each of us has a name
given by the seasons
and given by our blindness
Each of us has a name
given by the sea
and given by
our death.

Zelda (translated by Marcia Falk)

The Intention
Healing is both an exercise
and an understanding
and yet not of the will
nor of the intention
It is a wisdom
and a deeper knowledge
of the daily swing
of life and death
in all creation
There is defeat
to overcome

and acceptance of living
to be established
and always
there must be hope
Not hope of healing
but the hope which informs
the coming moment
and gives it reason
The hope which is each man's
    breath
the certainty of love
and of loving
Death may live
in the living
and healing rise
in the dying
for whom the natural end
is part of the gathering
and of the harvest
to be expected
To know healing is to know
that all life is one
and there is no beginning
and no end
To know healing
is to know that
all life is one
and there is no beginning
and no end
and the intention is loving.

Margaret Torrie

Autumn Psalm of Fearlessness
I am surrounded by a peaceful
    ebbing,
    as creation bows to the mystery
    of life;
    all that grows and lives must
    give up life,
    yet it does not really die.

131

As plants surrender their life,
    bending, brown and wrinkled,
    and yellow leaves of trees
    float to my lawn like parachute
        troops,
they do so in a sea of serenity.

I hear no fearful cries from
        creation,
    no screams of terror,
    as death daily devours
    once-green and growing life.
Peaceful and calm is autumn's
        swan song,
    for she understands
    that hidden in winter's death-
        grip
    is spring's openhanded,
    full-brimmed breath of life.

It is not a death rattle that sounds
    over fields and backyard fences;
    rather I hear a lullaby
    softly swaying upon the
        autumn wind.
Sleep in peace, all that lives;
    slumber secure, all that is
        dying,
    for in every fall there is the rise
    whose sister's name is spring.
                        Edward Hays

When we are weary and in need
    of strength,
When we are lost and sick at
    heart,
We remember him.

When we have a joy we crave to
    share

When we have decisions that are
    difficult to make
When we have achievements that
    are based on his
We remember him.

At the blowing of the wind and
    in the chill of winter
At the opening of the buds and
    in the rebirth of spring,
We remember him.

At the blueness of the skies and
    in the warmth of summer
At the rustling of the leaves and
    in the beauty of autumn,
We remember him.

At the rising of the sun and at its
    setting,
We remember him.

As long as we live, he too will
    live
For he is now a part of us,
As we remember him.
            from THE YIZKOR SERVICE, *adapted*

Last Lines
The following are the last lines my
sister Emily ever wrote:
                        (Charlotte Brontë)

No coward soul is mine,
No trembler in the world's storm-
    troubled sphere:
I see heaven's glories shine,
And faith shines equal, arming
    me from fear.

O God within my breast,
Almighty, ever-present Deity!

Life – that in me has rest,
As I – undying Life – have power
   in thee!

Vain are the thousand creeds
That move men's hearts:
   unutterably vain;
Worthless as withered weeds,
Or idlest froth amid the
   boundless main,

To waken doubt in one
Holding so fast by thine infinity;
So surely anchored on
The steadfast rock of immortality.

With wide-embracing love
Thy spirit animates eternal years,
Pervades and broods above,
Changes, sustains, dissolves,
   creates, and rears.

Though earth and man were
   gone,
And suns and universes ceased
   to be,
And thou were left alone,
Every existence would exist in
   thee.

There is not room for Death,
Nor atom that his might could
   render void:

Thou – thou art Being and
   Breath,
And what thou art may never be
   destroyed.

Emily Brontë

What is human life?
Life is a song – sing it.
Life is a game – play it.
Life is a challenge – meet it.
Life is a dream – realise it.
Life is a sacrifice – offer it.
Life is Love – enjoy it.

Sai Baba

A final thought:
When I am dead
Cry for me a little.
Think of me sometimes,
But not too much.
Think of me now and again
As I was in life,
At some moments it's pleasant to
   recall,
But not for long.
Leave me in Peace
And I shall leave you in peace.
And while you live,
Let your thoughts be with the
   living.

Traditional Indian Prayer

4. SUGGESTED BIBLICAL READINGS FOR FUNERAL/ MEMORIAL SERVICES

2 Samuel 1:25–27. How did the heroes fall in thick of battle

Job 14:1–9. Man, born of woman, has a short life, yet has his fill of sorrow

Job 19:21–27a. This I know, my avenger (redeemer) lives

Proverbs 31:16–31. In praise of a good woman

Ecclesiasticus 2:1–11. Fear of God in time of ordeal

Isaiah 25:6–9. He will destroy death forever

Isaiah 35:3–10. Sorrow and lament be ended

Isaiah 43:19. See, I am doing a new deed

Isaiah 60:20. Yahweh will be your everlasting light and your days of mourning will be ended

Isaiah 61:3. To comfort all those who mourn

Isaiah 65:17. For now I create a new heaven and a new earth

Lamentations 3:22. The favours of Yahweh are not all past, his kindnesses are not exhausted

Ezekiel 37:6. I am now going to make breath enter you and you will live

Daniel 12:1–3. Those who sleep in the dust of the earth shall wake

Wisdom 3:1–9. But the souls of the virtuous are in the hands of God

Wisdom 4:7–14. The virtuous man, though he die before his time, will find rest

Wisdom 5:15–16. But the virtuous live forever

Ecclesiastes 3:1–14. There is a season for everything

Ecclesiastes 7:1–14. The heart of the wise as in the house of mourning

Ecclesiastes 12:1–7. Remember your creator in the days of your youth

Psalms

16 – Yahweh, my heritage, my cup

23 – Yahweh is my Shepherd, I lack nothing

25 – To you Yahweh I lift up my soul, O my God

27 – In God's company there is no fear

31 – Prayer, in time of ordeal, for the bereaved

38 – Prayer in distress

41 – Happy the man who cares for the poor and the weak

43 – Lament of a Levite in exile

43 – Defend me, take up my cause

46 – God is on our side

88 – Lament for those who feel defeated

90 – I protect whoever knows my name

103 – As tenderly as a father treats his children

106 – Give thanks to Yahweh, for he is good, his love is everything

116 – I have faith, even when I say I am completely crushed

121 – I lift up my eyes to the mountains

130 – I wait for Yahweh, my soul waits for him

139 – Yahweh, you examine me and know me

143 – Yahweh, hear my prayer

145 – Yahweh acts only out of love

New Testament

Matthew 5:5. Happy are those who mourn for they shall be comforted

Matthew 11:25–30. The good news revealed to the simple

Matthew 18:1–5. Who is the greatest

Matthew 25:31–40. The last judgement

Matthew 28:1–10. Do not be afraid

Mark 5:22–23. The daughter of Jairus raised to life

Mark 10:13–16. Let the little children come to me

Mark 12:20–25. The power of faith – the resurrection of the dead

Luke 7:11–16. The son of the widow of Nain restored to life

Luke 12:35–40. On being ready for the master's return

Luke 23:33. The good thief. Today you will be with me in paradise

John 5:21–29. The father raises the dead, the son gives to whom he chooses

John 6:35–40. I am the bread of life

John 10:11–16. I am the good shepherd

John 11:21–27. If you had been here my brother would not have died

John 12:23–26. Now the hour has come for the son of man to be glorified

John 14:1–6. There are many rooms in my father's house

John 14:8–9. Because I live you will also live

John 15:9–17. As the father has loved me, so have I loved you

John 16:16. Jesus is to return – he has overcome the world

John 17:1–15. Jesus raised his eyes to heaven and said 'Father, the hour has come'

Acts 10:34–43. God does not have any favourites

Romans 5:1–10. Faith guarantees our sharing in the glory of God

Romans 6:3–11. Christ raised from the dead, we too might have a new life

Romans 8:11. If Christ is in you then your spirit is life itself

Romans 14:7–13. The life and

death of each of us has its influence on others

1 Corinthians 1:3–5. The sending of grace and peace

1 Corinthians 13:1–13. Faith, hope and love and the greatest of these is love

1 Corinthians 15:12–19. The facts and reassurance of the resurrection

1 Corinthians 15:20–22. But Christ had in fact been raised from the dead

1 Corinthians 15:45–58. If the soul has its own embodiment, so does the spirit have its own embodiment

2 Corinthians 1:3–5. A gentle father and the God of all consolation

2 Corinthians 4:7–14. Perplexed, but not in despair

2 Corinthians 5:15. He died for all

2 Corinthians 4:16. The inner man is renewed day by day

Ephesians 1:3–10. The triumph and supremacy of Christ

Philippians 3:8–21. I believe that nothing can happen without the knowing of Jesus

Philippians 3:17. My brothers be united in following my rule of life

Philippians 4:1–4, 7. Do not give way but remain faithful

Colossians 1:11–20. You will have in you the strength

Thessalonians 4:13–18. With such thoughts as these you should comfort each other

1 John 3:1–2. Live as God's children

1 John 4:7–12. My dear people, let us love one another

Revelation 7:9–17. God shall wipe away all tears from their eyes

Revelation 19:5–9. And all great and small shall revere him

Revelation 21:2–7. He will wipe away all the tears from their eyes, there will be no more death, and no more mourning or sadness or pain

5. SHORT READINGS

It is abundantly clear that this lifetime is a series of simultaneous deaths and births ... It is also clear that the farther one travels on the journey of life, the more births one will experience, and therefore the more deaths – the more joy and the more pain.

M. Scott Peck

Throughout our lives, death and birth repeat themselves. Many little deaths lead to many little births. We die to wombs and are born into worlds. But these worlds become larger wombs for us. We die to them and are born into larger worlds: our mother's womb, the breast, the nursery, the home, neighbourhood, family, school, each grade in school, friends, jobs, cities. We are like multistage rockets; each stage dies and falls away when its job is done, for its job is only to launch us forward.

Peter Kreeft

Sometimes, unexpectedly, grief and nostalgia overwhelm us, just when we thought we had dealt with our emotions. We should not feel guilty about this, nor feel that we are slipping backwards in the grieving process. When we do reach these seasons of desolation it is wise to remember that even

Nature has its progression of seasons – its winter as well as its summer; its autumn as well as its spring. And within each season is a special beauty, and some special indication of hope. When we are feeling nostalgic, we can indulge for a while in the nostalgic words of others who know well the pangs of longing.

Catherine Glen

The terrible fire of grief is an energetic furnace, refining character, personality, intellect, and soul. It is a catalyst for creation. What is created may be dreadful – a distorted, unapproachable monument to despair – or a distillation of experience that is wholesome, useful, bright, and even wise.

Peg Elliot Mayo

Ho Ka Hey! Follow me
Today is a good day to fight
Today is a good day to die.
Each morning the Oglala Sioux warrior said Ho Ka Hey (it's a good day to die), thus expressing a willingness to surrender to death at any time, fearlessly.

Chief Crazy Horse

Jesus, who never grew old, it is not easy for any of us who face old age. It is fine to be young, attractive, strong. Old age reminds us of weakness and dependence on others. But to be your disciple means accepting weakness and inter-dependence. Because of you we can rejoice in weakness in ourselves, and be tender to it in others.

Monica Furlong

Bereavement is the deepest initiation into the mysteries of human life, an initiation more searching and profound than even happy love. Love remembered and consecrated by grief belongs more clearly than the happy intercourse of friends to the eternal world; it has proved itself stronger than death.

Bereavement is the sharpest challenge to our trust in God; if faith can overcome this then there is no mountain which it cannot remove. And faith can overcome it. It brings the eternal world nearer to us and makes it seem more real.

Dean Inge

I say to my people who are dying:
Soon after you're dead – we're not sure how
long – but not long – you'll be united with
the most ecstatic love you've ever known.
As one of the best things in your life was

a human love, this will last forever.

Cardinal Basil Hume OSB

If anyone were to ask me, 'What's the most important thing in life for you?' I think I would probably have to answer in a single word, 'Friends'. Of course some friends are more important than others; but quite a number are very important to me. And if someone were to say to me, 'But as a priest, isn't God more important to you than any of your friends?' I'd have to say that God is above all and through all and in all; and it's in and through my friends that I think I have learnt, and still do learn, most about God and receive most from Him.

Eric James

We do not wholly die at our deaths: we have mouldered away gradually long before. Faculty after faculty, interest after interest, attachment after attachment disappear: we are torn from ourselves while living, year after year sees us no longer the same, and death only consigns the last fragment of what we were to the grave. That we should wear out by slow stages, and dwindle at last into nothing, is not wonderful, when even in our prime our strongest impressions leave little trace for the moment, and we are the creatures of petty circumstance.

William Hazlitt

The first Christians lived face to face with death but their final death enabled them to die daily to their immediate sufferings and to live in the power of resurrection life. For many of us today, the refusal to look death in the face robs us of the reality of that resurrection experience. Tidying up the affairs of a person who has died puts new perspective on all that person lived for. What will be saved out of it all? The money – of no value to him now. The property – standing empty. The clothes – to be cast away. But the faith and the hope and the love by which he lived – these surely are vindicated, these are of eternal value, these are saved as his life reaches its ultimate meaning beyond the grave, in the salvation that belongs to our God.

Pauline Webb

I have got my leave. Bid me farewell my brothers. I bow to you all and take my departure. Here I give back the keys of my door – and I give up all claims to my house. I only ask for last kind words from you. We were neighbours for long, but I received more than I could give. Now the day has dawned and the lamp that lit my dark corner is out. A summons has come and I am ready for my journey.

Rabindranath Tagore

Our dying has a quality of healing when all about us are touched by the recognition of the preciousness of each moment. Our dying is a healing when all that has been unsaid is touched with forgiveness and love, when all imagined unpaid obligations of the past are resolved in mercy and loving kindness.

Stephen Levine

I believe you died in God's will, and that you are eternal, but of your place and condition I know nothing, and I do not speculate about it ... if I am ever in any sense of the word to *know* you again, there will be no jealousies and angers and arrogances and impatiences, but only joy. And sorrow and pain shall be no more, neither sighing, but life everlasting.

And if such things are never to be, then I give thanks, for during the writing of these words, I have come out of the valley of darkness.

Did you intercede for me?

Alan Paton

There is time of weeping and there is time of laughing. But as you see, he setteth the weeping time before, for that is the time of this wretched world and the laughing time shall come after in heaven. There is also a time of sowing, and a time of reaping too. Now must we in this world sow, that we may in the other world reap: and in this short sowing time of this weeping world, must we water our seed with the showers of our tears, and then shall we have in heaven a merry laughing harvest for ever.

St Thomas More

The question is not how to survive but how to thrive with passion, compassion, humour and style. Only have in your life that which supports and celebrates your aims and purposes and detach immediately from everything which doesn't.

Round my neck I wear a metal tag engraved with the words of Maya Angelou: 'The question is not how to survive, but how to thrive with passion, compassion and style.'

Maya Angelou

North American Indian Funeral Chant

I am not there
Do not stand at my grave and
  weep
I am not there, I do not sleep.
I am a thousand winds that
  blow,
I am the diamond glint on snow.
I am the sunlight on ripened
  grain,
I am the gentle autumn rain.
When you wake in the morning
  hush
I am the swift, uplifting rush
Of quiet birds in circling flight,
I am the soft starlight at
  night.
Do not stand at my grave and cry,
I am not there – I did not die.

(found in the belongings of Stephen Cummins, a Portsmouth soldier killed in Northern Ireland)

6. LONG READINGS

Life and Death

While living, identify with life; when dying, with death. Do not give way, do not desire. Life and death are the essential being of Buddha. If therefore you abandon life and death you will lose; and if you attach yourself either to life or to death, you will lose. Do not hate and do not desire; do not think and do not speak of these things. Forget your body and spirit and put them in the Buddha's hands and let him guide you. Then without striving for an end you will reach freedom and Buddhahood. The way there is easy. Shun evil, do nothing about life and death, show mercy to all living things, show respect to your superiors and sympathy to your inferiors. Do not like or dislike. Live without worry or speculation. That is the only way to Buddhahood.

Dogen

The process of dying, I would suggest, is not unlike the process of being born, and this is, perhaps, a helpful way of approaching it. Here we are in the 'womb' of this world, the limitations of time and space surrounding us and hemming us in until finally our journey through this world leads s out and beyond and into an altogether new and different future, a future about which there will surely be that same sense of curiosity, excitement and adventure as when we entered this life.

Of course there is bound to be sadness and sorrow for those left behind, and I would in no way wish to minimise that. But for our loved one who has gone before us, there is now true freedom, real fulfilment and the joy of discovering that we are still one in the risen and living Lord, the one who was dead and behold he is alive for evermore.

David Hope

Life and death are one, even as
    the river and the sea are one.
In the depth of your hopes and
    desires lies your silent
    knowledge of the beyond;
And like seeds dreaming beneath
    the snow your heart dreams of
    spring.
Trust the dreams, for in them
    is hidden the gate to
    eternity . . .

For what is to die but to stand
    naked in the wind and to melt
    it into the sun?
And what is it to cease breathing
    but to free the breath from its

141

restless tides, that it may rise
and expand and seek God
unencumbered?
Only when you drink from the
river of silence shall you
indeed sing.
And when you have reached the
mountain top, then you shall
begin to climb. + *these*
And when the earth shall claim
your limbs, then shall you
truly dance.

Kahlil Gibran

When I think of death, and of late
the idea has come with alarming
frequency, I seem at peace with
the idea that a day will dawn when
I will no longer be among those
living in this valley of strange
humors. I can accept the idea of
my own demise, but I am unable
to accept the death of anyone else.
I find it impossible to let a friend
or relative go into that country
of no return. Disbelief becomes
my close companion, and anger
follows in its wake.

I answer the heroic question
'Death, where is thy sting?' with
'It is here in my heart and mind
and memories.'

I am besieged with painful awe
at the vacuum left by the dead.
Where did she go? Where is she
now? Are they, as the poet James
Weldon Johnson said, 'resting in
the bosom of Jesus'? If so, what
about my Jewish loves, my
Japanese dears, and my Muslim
darlings. Into whose bosom are
they cuddled? There is always,
lurking quietly, the question of
what certainty is there that I, even
I, will be gathered into the gentle
arms of the Lord. I start to suspect
that only with such blessed assurance will I be able to allow death
its duties.

I find surcease from the
entanglement of questions only
when I concede that I am not
obliged to know everything. In a
world where many desperately
seek to know all the answers, it is
not very popular to believe, and
then state, I do not need to know
all things. I remind myself that it
is sufficient that I know what I
know and know that without
believing that I will always know
what I know or that what I
know will always be true.

Also, when I sense myself filling
with rage at the absence of a
beloved, I try as soon as possible to
remember that my concerns and
questions, my efforts and answers
should be focused on what I did or
can learn from my departed love.
What legacy was left which can
help me in the art of living a good
life?

If I employ the legacies of my
late beloveds, I am certain death
will take itself and me as well.

Maya Angelou

O Mother-Father God, ever
loving and ever living, the final

reality in which all souls find their completion, rest and fulfillment, we pray for him whom you know and love far more deeply than we can even imagine. Give him your light and love for which he sought so fervently. In your mercy heal, strengthen, enlighten, and guide him as he enters the unbounded and mysterious vistas of eternity. May his immortal being reveal more and more the infinite potential of wisdom, joy, and compassion with which you endow the human soul. May he know the intimate fellowship of the children of God and become an ambassador of your caring and peace to all dimensions of your universe.

O Gracious One, let him know how much we love and miss his physical presence and long to be with him. Grant that he may be allowed to guide and guard our journey until we meet in that condition where partings cease. Until then give us a sense of his loving presence. Heal all his wounds inflicted by an insensitive and unconscious society. Let us minister in any way we can to his growth, peace, and joy. Let us do nothing that keeps us from fellowship together in the communion of saints. We ask this of you, a loving God who created us, saw our misery, came among us, suffered with us, suffered for us, and by rising again opened to us the portals of eternal life. Amen.

Morton Kelsey

My Son at the Door of Death
Fear not for me. I'm not afraid.
A new adventure awaits me.
A new more brilliant being
Is about to birth
Into a different space and time.
The garden of heaven and those
　abiding there
Are calling me insistently. They
　want me soon.
They sing of my courage and
　frustration,
Of years of seeking, relentless
　searching . . .
So many roads that petered out
In scorching desert and burning
　sand
And still I kept on, was guided.
These voices promise
To answer all my questions
With love unbounded, limitless.
They offer intimacy, closeness, far
　richer
Than I had dared to hope for,
　and wisdom, too,
And living water drawn from the
　deepest well
That holds the secret mysteries
　safe
From vain and curious wanderers.
The voices also sing of love and
　loving,
Of giving all I had and only at
　this moment
Knowing that my arrow struck its
　mark.

Do not hold me back. I'll be with
  you still
In fuller measure than I've ever
  given.
The sun is rising from the sea
As one by one the stars are lost
  in light.
The broken has been mended.
I can be loved and love.
It is time to go.
Pushed beyond the limits
Of death and pain and hope,
I find the real
Eternal Love.

Morton Kelsey

We are one people, one community and the death of one is the
concern of all. In the face of death
man can achieve grandeur, but if
he turns his back on death he
remains a child, clinging to a land
of make-believe. For death is not
the ending of the pattern of life's
unwinding, but a necessary inter-
ruption. Through the painful
work of grieving we rediscover the
past and weave it afresh into a new
reality.

Our aim cannot be to cancel
out the past, to try to forget, but
to ensure that the strength and
meaning which gave beauty to the
old pattern is remembered and
reinterpreted in the pattern now
emerging. Every man must die but
the world is permanently changed
by each man's existence. . . . There
is no easy way through the long
valley but we have faith in the

ability of each one to find his own
way, given time and the encouragement of the rest of us.

Colin Murray Parkes

Yet death is but a transition. We
pass through a door from one
space to another. It is a moment
of nature, so that we would do
better to use the present participle,
'dying'. We die but to be reborn.
And exactly how we go through
that last door, how we die, will
depend on how we respond to the
many hourly, daily, yearly experiences of dying that we encounter
in our lives, how we respond to
the dying of a hope, a dream, a
friendship, an ambition, a passion.
If we learn how to live through
each of these miniature deaths,
each lessening of the ego, then
each of them will become a resurrection, and so we shall come at
last to those ten thousand several
doors with joy and gratitude,
humility and trust. If, on our
journey down the years, we do
this, then we shall also hear,
increasingly nearer, that music
from another room which is the
life that is beyond and yet is all
about us even now. And if, con-
tinually, hourly, daily, yearly, we
learn how to die and be reborn,
then we shall find that after long
searching a door opens and there
is a way ahead when we had
thought no door would ever open
for us. It may not be the door we

expected, nor the door we would have chosen for ourselves, but it has opened and we have but to enter.

James Roose-Evans

We bereaved are not alone. We belong to the largest company in all the world – the company of those who have known suffering. When it seems that our sorrow is too great to be borne, let us think of the great family of the heavy-hearted into which our grief has given us entrance, and inevitably, we will feel about us their arms, their sympathy, their understanding.

Believe, when you are most unhappy, that there is something for you to do in the world. So long as you can sweeten another's pain, life is not vain.

Helen Keller

Treya, my guardian angel, you were a star on earth and gave us all warmth and light, but every star must die to be born again, this time in the heavens above, dwelling with the eternal lightness of the soul. I know you are dancing upon the clouds right now, and I'm lucky enough to feel your joy, feel your smile. I look at the sky and I know you're shining, with your brilliant, radiant soul.

I love you Treya and I know I'll miss you here, but I'm so happy for you! You have shed your body and your pains, and are able to dance the dance of true life, and that is the life of the soul. I can dance with you in my dreams, and in my heart. So, you are not dead, your soul still lives, lives on a higher plane, and in your loved ones' hearts.

You've taught me the most
    important lesson, what life
    and love is.
Love is complete and sincere
    respect for another being . . .
It is the ecstasy of the true self . . .
Love extends beyond all planes
    and is limitless . . .
After a million lives, and a
    million deaths it still lives . . .
And it only dwells in the heart
    and soul . . .
Life is of the soul, and of nothing
    else . . .
Love and laughter ride with it,
    but so do pain and anguish . . .

Ken Wilber

7. HYMNS

	N.E.H.	H.O.N.	C.H.
Abide with me	331	6	–
All hope in God is founded	333	15	–
All things bright and beautiful	264	21	13
As the deer pants for water	–	39	–
Amazing grace	–	27	19
Be thou my vision, O Lord of my heart	339	56	35
Blest are the pure in heart	341	63	36
Come down O love divine	137	90	49
Come holy ghost our souls inspire	138	92	–
Contakion for the dead	526	–	–
Dear lord and father of mankind	353	106	60
For all the saints	197	134	77
God is love let heaven adore him	364	–	–
Guide me, O thou great redeemer	368	188	104
Hail, gladdening light	–	189	–
He who would valiant be	372	205	119
How great thou art	–	–	380
Immortal, invisible, God only wise	377	242	134
Just as I am	294	–	–
Jesus lover of my soul	383	261	150
Let saints on earth in concert sing	396	297	–
Lift high the cross	–	–	303
Lord of all hopefulness	239	313	181
Lord for the years	–	310	–
Make a channel of your peace	–	328	189
Morning has broken	237	337	196
Now thank we all our God	413	–	–
O love that will not let me go	–	384	–
Seek ye first the kingdom of God	–	442	593
Take my life and let it be	246	464	608
The day thou gavest Lord is ended	252	475	303

The God of Abrah'm praise	148	478	–
The Lord's my shepherd	459	490	312
The strife is o'er, the battle done	119	495	–
Thine be the glory	120	503	622

N.E.H. – New English Hymnal
H.O.N. – Hymns Old and New
C.H. – Celebrational Hymnal

8. CLASSICAL MUSIC

J. S. Bach	Selections from St Matthew Passion
	'Jesu Joy of Man's Desiring'
	'Sheep may safely graze'
	Toccata and Fugue in D Minor
Samuel Barber	Adagio for Strings
L. van Beethoven	Symphony No.6 'Pastoral', last movement
	Symphony No.9 'Choral', last movement
Benjamin Britten	Simple Symphony, 3rd movement
Anton Bruckner	'Kyrie' from Mass in E Minor
William Byrd	'The Souls of the Righteous'
Frederic Chopin	Funeral March
Aaron Copeland	Fanfare for the Common Man
W. Croft	'I am the resurrection and the life'
Frederick Delius	The walk to the Paradise Garden
Antonin Dvořák	'Ascension' from New World Symphony
	'Going Home' from New World Symphony
Edward Elgar	'Nimrod' from Enigma Variations
	Introduction and Allegro for Strings
	'Go forth upon thy journey, O Christian soul'
	'Ave Verum Corpus' (Hail True Body)
Gabriel Fauré	'In Paradisum' from Requiem
	'Libera Me' from Requiem
	'Pie Jesu' from Requiem
	'Sanctus' from Requiem
Henryk Górecki	The Symphony of Sorrowful Songs, No.3
C. F. Ground	'O Divine Redeemer Repentir'
	Sanctus Messe Solennelle de Sainte Cecile
G. F. Handel	'Comfort ye my people' from The Messiah
	'I know that my redeemer liveth' from The Messiah
	'The trumpet shall sound' from The Messiah
	'Zadok the priest', George II's Coronation Anthem
F. J. Haydn	'Seven last words of our saviour'
John Ireland	'Greater love hath no man than this'

Gustav Mahler	Symphony No.5, Adagietto
	'Song of the earth' (Third song, about youth)
Felix Mendelssohn	'Be thou faithful unto death'
	'Hear my prayer'
	'O rest in the Lord' from Elijah
Thomas Morley	Nunc Dimitis 'Lord now lettest thy servant depart in peace'
W. A. Mozart	'Kyrie' from Mass in C Minor
	Ave Verum Corpus (Hail True Body)
Johann Pachelbel	Canon and Gigue in D
C. H. H. Parry	'There is an old belief'
Giovanni Pergolesi	Stabat Mater, 'Duetto grave'
Giacomo Puccini	'Vissi d'Arte' from Tosca
Henry Purcell	'Dido's lament' from Dido and Aeneas
	'When I am laid in earth' from Dido and Aeneas
Ariel Ramirez	Gloria Missa Criolla
John Rutter	'God be in my head'
Franz Schubert	'The Lord is my shepherd' (23rd Psalm)
	'Ave Maria'
C. V. Stanford	Justorum Animae, 'The souls of the righteous'
Igor Stravinsky	The Finale from The Firebird
Vangelis	1492 Symphony
Ralph Vaughan-Williams	The turtle dove
	The lark ascending
	Fantasia on a theme of Thomas Tallis
Giuseppe Verdi	Requiem
Louis Vierne	Finale, Symphonie No. 1
	Largetto, Symphonie No.6
Antonio Vivaldi	'Spring' and 'Autumn' from The Four Seasons
Richard Wagner	'Isolde's Lament' from Tristan and Isolde
	'Liebestod' from Tristan and Isolde
	Siegfried Funeral March from Götterdämmerung
S. S. Wesley	'Thou will keep him in perfect peace'
William Walton	'Drop, drop slow tears' – a litany
Charles-Marie Widor	Toccata in F
	Londonderry Air

9. NON-CLASSICAL MUSIC

Artist/Songwriter	Title	Label
Abba	I have a dream	Epic
Shirley Bassey	Ballad of the sad old man	EMI
	I did it my way	EMI
Kate Bush	Moments of please	EMI
Toni Childs	Heaven's Gate	Polygram
	The dead are dancing	Polygram
Eric Clapton	Tears in Heaven	Duck
Leonard Cohen	Bird on the Wire	Sony
Communards	For a friend	London/Lon
Enya	China Roses	WEA
	Evening falls	WEA
	On my way home	WEA
	On your shore	WEA
	Once you had gold	WEA
Gloria Estefan	Let's speak the same language	Sony
Agnetha Faltskog	Wrap your arms round me	Epic
Aretha Franklin	Walk in the light	WEA
Marvin Gaye	His eyes are on the sparrows	Polygram
Gerry and the Pacemakers	You'll never walk alone	Columbia
Michael Jackson	You are not alone	Sony
Elton John	Candle in the wind	Rockett
	Song for Guy	Rockett
	The last song	Rockett
	Sacrifice	Rockett
Gladys Knight	The way we try to remember	Buddah
Patti Labelle	Love never dies	Sony
La Cage aux Folles	I did it my way	Telstar
Annie Lennox	Little bird	RCA
	Why?	RCA
Freddie Mercury	The show must go on	Parlophone
Bette Midler	Shiver me timbers	WEA
	Wind beneath my wings	Atlantic
	The Rose	Atlantic
Pet Shop Boys	Always on My Mind	EMI (Manhatten)
Edith Piaf	No regrets	EMI
Cole Porter	Everybody hurts	Warner

150

Prince	Adore	WEA
Queen	These are the days of our lives	EMI
REM	Everybody hurts	Warner
Frank Sinatra	My Way	Reprise
Jimmy Somerville	For a friend	Parlophone
Squeeze	Is that love?	A & M
Donna Summer	I feel love	Casablanca
Sweet People	And the birds were singing	Polydor
Tina Turner	The Best	Capitol

PART THREE: Information

1. PALLIATIVE CARE ORGANISATIONS

Association of Chartered Physiotherapists in Oncology and Palliative Care St Catherine's Hospice, 137 Scalby Road, Scarborough. YO12 6TB *Tel*: 01723 351421.
Mainly for physiotherapists working either in oncology wards of general hospitals, in hospices or in the community but other professions welcome as associate members. They also offer membership to health professionals overseas.

Association for Palliative Medicine 11 Westwood Road, Southampton SO17 1DL *Tel*: 01703 672888 *Fax*: 01703 672888.
Open to all doctors, the association's objectives are to encourage the principles of good palliative medicine and promote education and research and self audit in the speciality – it also advises on career and medical staffing matters.

Palliative and Continuing Care Centre (Trent Region) Sykes House, Little Common Lane, Abbey Lane, Sheffield S11 9EL *Tel*: 0114 262 0174.
The Centre co-ordinates educational and research initiatives in terminal care.

Royal College of Nursing (RCN) Palliative Nursing Group 20 Cavendish Square, London W1M OAB *Tel*: 0171–409 3333/872 0840 *Fax*: 0171–495 6104.
Provides a forum for nurses engaged in palliative care to improve patient care by addressing issues of palliative nursing practice, education, research and management. Membership is open to RCN members working in palliative care as well as nurses caring for people in any diagnostic group requiring palliative care. The Group publishes a newsletter and holds an annual conference.

Scottish Partnership Agency for Palliative and Cancer Care 1a Cambridge Street, Edinburgh EH1 2DY *Tel*: 0131–229 0538 *Fax*: 0131–228 2967.
Brings together voluntary and statutory bodies concerned with palliative and cancer care services in Scotland. It facilitates communication among

services and with the Government, enabling them to work together for the development and improvement of palliative and cancer care services in Scotland.

2. OVERSEAS PALLIATIVE CARE ORGANISATIONS

Canadian Palliative Care Association 5 Blackburn Avenue, Ottawa, Ontario, K1N 8A2, Canada *Tel*: 00 1 613 230 3343 *Fax*: +230 4376.
The Association offers leadership in pursuit of excellence in the care of people approaching death. Publishes the Canadian Directory for Community-based and Hospital Palliative Care Services, and recently published 'Palliative Care: towards a consensus in standardised principles of practice'. Sponsors biennial education conference.

European Association for Palliative Care National Cancer Institute, Milan, Via Venezian 1, 20133 Milan, Italy *Tel*: 00 39 2 2390792 *Fax*: +2 70600462.
A multi-disciplinary Association established in 1988 to increase awareness and spread knowledge of palliative care in Europe. The Association publishes quarterly the EAPC Journal and Newsletter in English and French: subscription details available from Hayward Medical Publications Tel: 01608 645564.

Hospice Education Institute 190 Westbrook Road, Essex, Connecticut 06426 1511, USA. *Tel*: 00 1 860 767 1620 *Fax*: +767 2746.
Offers continuing education to health professionals and consultation to health care organisatiohs. Free telephone advice and support service (Hospicelink) (800 331 1620) for members of the public and health professionals seeking information on, and referral to hospice and palliative care units throughout the USA. Also maintains a directory of US hospices and palliative care units and a database of UK grief support services.

Hospice New Zealand PO Box 12–481, Wellington, New Zealand. *Tel*: 00 64 6 499 0266 *Fax*: +4 473 3554.
Co-ordinating body for the hospice movement in New Zealand. Promotes the principles of hospice palliative care through education for health professionals and volunteers, quarterly newsletter, annual conferences and national standards.

Irish Association For Palliative Care Marymount Hospice, St

Patrick's Hospital, Wellington Road, Cork, Ireland. *Tel*: 00 353 (0) 21 507110 *Fax*: +507110.

This association provides a network for people involved in palliative care through education, support and research. The association also monitors the overall development of services in Ireland.

National Hospice Organisation 1901 North Moore Street, Suite 901, Arlington, Virginia 22209, USA. *Administration*: 1 703 243 59000 *Fax*: +525 5762.

NHO provides educational programmes, technical assistance, publications, advocacy and hospice referral services to the general public (*Tel*: 1 800 658 8898). Annual publication 'The Guide to the Nation's Hospices' lists every known hospice program throughout the USA.

World Health Organisation 1211 Geneva 27, Switzerland *Tel*: 00 41 22 791 3477 *Fax*: +791 0746.

Assists the WHO's member states in the areas of cancer and palliative care: co-ordinates palliative care and cancer activities world-wide, develops policies for the implementation of good palliative care practice.

3. CARE GROUPS

Association of Crossroads Care Attendant Schemes   10 Regent Place, Rugby, Warwickshire CV21 2PN   *Tel*: 01788 573653   *Fax*: 01788 565498.
Trained carers who take over from the regular carer completely in looking after a disabled person at home, so as to give the carer a break.

Care for the Carers Council   143 High Street, Lewes, East Sussex BN7 1XT   *Tel*: 01273 476819.
Advice, information and support, primarily in the East Sussex area.

Care Foundation (The)   Michael Tetley Hall, Sandhurst Road, Tunbridge Wells, Kent TN2 3JS   *Tel*: 01892 544877.
A registered charity which funds Hospice at Home and the Information Centre based at Sevenoaks Hospital which provides information to the general public for people living with serious illness, their relatives, carers and friends.

Carer's National Association   Ruth Pitter House, 20–25 Glasshouse Yard, London EC1A 4JS   *Tel*: 0171–490 8818   *Helpline*: 0171–490 8898 (1–4pm weekdays)   *Fax*: 0171–490 8824.
Information, support and bereavement counselling for people who care for sick, disabled or frail elderly relatives or friends. Publishes free general information leaflets. Branches and support groups can give local information and mutual help.

4. HOSPICE INFORMATION

ANANDA NETWORK   Buddhist Hospice Trust, P.O. Box 123, Ashford, Kent TN24 9TF   *Tel*: 0181 789 6170.
Although Buddhist-based, companionship is offered to the dying or the bereaved of any religion or those with no religion. At the moment it is a network of people rather than a building. Caroline Sherwood (Parsonage Farm Cottage, Stoney Stratton, Shepton Mallet BA4 6EA, *Tel*: 01749 830827) offers counselling and teaching by phone or mail for people wanting help with fear of death or associated issues.

Association of Hospice Administrators   North Devon Hospice Care Trust, Deer Park, Deer Park Road, Barnstaple, Devon EX32 0HU *Tel*: 01271 44248   *Fax*: 01271 71995.
Open to Principal administrators of independent hospice units and teams. Holds annual conferences, workshops and regional meetings.

Association of Hospice Chaplains   St Elizabeth's Hospice, 565 Foxhall Road, Ipswich IP3 8LX   *Tel*: 01473–727776   *Fax*: 01773 274717.
Provides training and support for clergy involved (full-time or part-time) in palliative and terminal care. In addition to a national residential conference held each spring, induction courses are held from time to time for those taking chaplaincy posts in hospices.

Association of Hospice Social Workers   East Cheshire Hospice, Millbank Drive, Macclesfield SK10 3BL   *Tel*: 01625 610364   *Fax*: 01625 612611.
The Association unites social workers working in hospices and hospice teams in hospitals or community. It seeks to promote professional development through an annual workshop and regional meetings, and workshops on current issues of importance.

Association of Hospice Voluntary Service Co-ordinators   Nightingale Continuing Care Unit, 117a London Road, Derby DE1 2QS *Tel*: 01332 254905   *Fax*: 01332 298813.
The Association aims to represent and support nationally all voluntary

service co-ordinators who are engaged in organising and co-ordinating volunteers in Hospice and palliative services.

Buddhist Hospice Trust   5 Grayswood Point, Roehampton, London SW15 4BT   *Tel*: 0181–789 6170
To request an Ananda Network volunteer telephone 0181–789 6170. Provides emotional support and spiritual care for those who are dying or bereaved from within a Buddhist perspective: publishes a bi-annual journal and offers seminars and study weekends. Also offers a nation-wide network of Buddhist volunteers, the Ananda Network, who will visit the dying and bereaved.

Forum of Chairmen of Independent Hospices   Acorns Children's Hospice Trust, 12 Middleton Hall Road, Cotteridge, Birmingham B30 1BY   *Tel*: 0121 628–0210   *Fax*: 0121–628 0211.
Provides information and support to trustees of independent hospices. It holds conferences twice yearly and provides advice and assistance for member hospices on an informal basis.

Help the Hospices   34–44 Britannia Street, London WC1X 9JG
Tel: 0171–278 5668   *Fax*: 0171–278 1021.
Grant-giving charity to help hospices with funding for education and training, equipment, commissioning grants. It runs and supports courses and conferences in the fields of palliative care, bereavement counselling, hospice management, managing volunteers, fund-raising. It does not support major construction work or the routine running costs of established units.

Hospice Arts   The Forbes Trust, 9 Artillery Lane, London E1 7LP
Tel: 0171–377 8484   *Fax*: 0171–377 0032.
A national charity established by the Forbes Trust and Help the Hospices to develop creative and therapeutic arts activities for hospice patients in the UK. Offers advice, information and contacts to any Hospice organisation wishing to establish or develop an arts programme. Correspondence should be addressed to The Director.

Hospice Information Service   St Christopher's Hospice, 51 Lawrie Park Road, Sydenham, London SE26 6DZ   *Tel*: 0181–778 9252
Fax: 0181–659 8680   *email*: 101377.77@compuserve.com.
Acts as a world-wide link to encourage sharing of information and

161

experience amongst those involved in palliative care services in UK and overseas. Publishes listings of job opportunities and of educational and training courses in palliative care and bereavement, and a quarterly newsletter, 'The Hospice Bulletin'. Also produces annual publication – 'Directory of hospice services in UK and Ireland and Hospice Worldwide – excluding North America and Australia'. Telephoned and written enquiries are welcomed from the public and from professionals.

Hospice in the Weald   Michael Tetley Hall, Sandhurst Road, Tunbridge Wells, Kent TN2 3JS   *Tel*: 01892 544877.
A professional team of specialists in palliative care – medical consultant, nurses, social workers and volunteers offering advice, support, counselling and bereavement support to patients with advanced cancer, MND or AIDS and their families. Referrals are accepted from GPs and consultants. The 24 hour service is offered to patients at home, in hospital or in residential or nursing homes. Day care is provided on Wednesdays and Fridays with holistic therapies.

Hospice Nurse Managers' Forum   Edenhall Marie Curie Home, 11 Lyndhurst Gardens, Hampstead, London NW3 5NS   *Tel*: 0171–794 0066.
The Forum is a forum of the Management Association at the Royal College of Nursing in the United Kingdom. It provides for nurses in hospice management to meet to consider matters relevant to their sphere of specialist nursing.

National Association of Hospice/Palliative Day Care Leaders   79 Elm Grove, Woburn Sands, Milton Keynes MK17 8QA   *Tel:/Fax*: 01908 583502.
Provides a network for Day Care Leaders, both locally and nationally, through education and support and promotes good practice within the membership. Organises an annual meeting and produces a newsletter.

National Council for Hospice and Specialist Palliative Care Services   59 Bryanston Street, London W1A 2AZ   *Tel*: 0171–1153 *Fax*: 0171–724 4341.
Acts as the co-ordinating and representative organisation for hospice and palliative care services in England, Wales and Northern Ireland. It represents the views and interests of hospice and palliative care services

to Government Health Authorities, the media and statutory and voluntary national agencies. It provides advice and facilitates the sharing of knowledge, information and experience. Convenes Working Party on Clinical Guidelines in Palliative Care. Publishes quarterly newsletter (Information Exchange) and a series of Occasional Papers.

Nurses Managing Hospices and Specialist Palliative Care Services   St Peter's Hospice, St Agnes Avenue, Knowle, Bristol BS4 2DU   *Tel*: 0117–977 4605   *Tel*: 0117–977 9676.
The Forum forms part of the Nurses in Management Group at the RCN of the UK and it provides opportunities for nurses engaged in the management of hospices and specialist palliative care services to meet together to consider matters relevant to their specialist sphere of nursing and management.

5. CHILDREN/YOUNG PERSONS' INFORMATION

Acorns Children's Hospice Trust   103 Oak Tree Lane, Selly Oak, Birmingham B2 6HZ   *Hospice*: 0121 414 1741   *Administration*: 0121 628 0210.
Provides project development support and operational planning services for children's hospice facilities.

Alder Centre   Royal Liverpool Children's Hospital, Alder Hey, Eaton Road, Liverpool L12 2AP   *Tel*: 0151 228 4811.
A national organisation for all those affected by the death of a child, both families and professionals. Evening helpline staffed by parents and volunteers, on a separate number. *Tel*: 0151 228 9759.

Association for Children with Life-threatening or Terminal Conditions and their Families (ACT)   65 St Michael's Hill, Bristol BS2 8DZ   *Tel*: 0117–922 1556   *Fax*: 0117–930 4707.
A national resource and information service for families and health care professionals involved in caring for children with life-threatening and terminal illness. The organisation is concerned with representing the needs of children and families and promoting models of good care throughout the UK. Act has a multidisciplinary membership.

Cancer Help Centre Grove House   Cornwallis Grove, Clifton, Bristol BS8 4PG   *Tel*: 0117 974 3216   *Fax*: 0117 923 9184.
Offers a holistic – dealing with the whole person – healing programme (to complement medical treatment) including relaxation, counselling, healing, nutrition, visualisation and meditation. Patients can attend for one day or a residential week. Education programmes for health professionals.

Child Bereavement Trust   Harleyford Estate, Henley Road, Marlowe, Bucks SL7 2DX   *Tel*: 01628 488101.

Child Death Helpline   Great Ormond Street Hospital, Bereavement Services Department, Great Ormond Street, London WC1N 3JH   *Administration*: 0171–829 86850   *Fax*: 0171–813 8516   *Helpline*: 0800 282986 (Mondays and Thursdays, 7 pm to 10 pm).

The Child Death helpline is operated from Great Ormond Street and the Alder Hey Children's Hospital. It is staffed by bereaved parents and it is a confidential helpline for anyone affected by the death of a child.

Childline   *Tel*: 0800 1111 24 hour service.
Young people can talk about anything.

The Cot Death Society   1 Browning Close, Thatcham, Newbury, Berkshire RG18 3EF   *Helpline*: 01635 861771.

Foundation for the Study of Infant Deaths   14 Halkin Street, London SW1X 7DP   *Administration*: 0171–235 0965   *Helpline*: 0171–235 1721 (24 hours).
This organisation is particularly concerned and interested in research into cot deaths. There are groups around the country. Counselling for parents bereaved in this way is provided, or parents can be put in touch with each other for mutual support.

Heart Line Association   *Tel*: 01795 539864.
Support group for parents of children with heart disease. There is also a bereavement support group.

Helping Young People with Cancer   A leaflet produced by Cancer Relief Macmillan Fund lists a range of organisations which can help young people with cancer. Available from CRMF, 15–19 Britten Street, London SW3 3TZ   *Tel*: 0171–351 7811.
Details of your local paediatric Macmillan Nursing Service can be obtained from the National Coordinator for Cancer Relief Macmillan Fund Head Office.   *Tel*: 0171–351 7811.

MAC Helpline   *Tel*: 0880 591028.
A freephone information and support service for young people affected by cancer.

Miscarriage Association   Clayton Hospital, Northgate, Wakefield WF1 3JS   *Helpline*: 01924 200799.
Gives information, help and support after a miscarriage. For information pack, enclose large s.a.e.

165

Parents Anonymous   8 Manor Gardens, London N7 6LA   *Tel*: 0171 263 8918.
Crisis support and counselling for parents of children who are critically ill in hospital and for parents and family who have lost a child through sudden death.

Parents Lifeline   Station House, 73d, Stapleton Hall Road, London N4 3QF   *Tel*: 0171–263 8918.
Offers crisis support and counselling for parents of children who are critically ill in hospital. Also offers free counselling for parents and siblings who have recently experienced the sudden death of a child.

REACT   73 Whitehall Park Road, London W4 3NB   *Tel*: 0181–995 8188.
A charity to assist children with life-threatening diseases and their families by grants to meet individual needs, by encouraging education and by sponsoring research into the care of such children. Also provides up to 50 holidays a year as well as a wide range of services including the provision of medical and domestic equipment.

The Rainbow Trust   Rainbow House, 47 Eastwick Drive, Great Bookham, Surrey KT23 3TU   *Tel*: 01372 453309.
Offers family-centred, respite and domiciliary care for terminally ill children.

Support Around Termination for Abnormality (SATFA)   National Office, 73 Charlotte Street, London W1P 1LB   *Helpline*: 0171–631 0285   *Administration*: 0171–631 0280.
Offers support and information to parents undergoing antenatal testing through diagnosis and decision making. Long-term support is available to those who decide to terminate.

The Starlight Foundation   8a Bloomsbury Square, London WC1A 2LP   *Tel*: 0171–430 1642.
Aims to grant the wishes of children who are critically, chronically or terminally ill. Age range 4–18 years.

The Stillbirth and Neonatal Death Society (SANDS)   28 Portland Place, London W1N 4DE   *Helpline*: 0171–436 5881.
Self-help organisation for those who have had stillborn babies. They

befriend, not counsel. National network of groups and contacts throughout the country.

Twin And Multiple Births Association (TAMBA) PO Box 30, Little Sutton, South Wirral L66 1TH *Administration*: 0151–348 0020 *Helpline*: 01732 868000.
Organises bereavement support group offering parent-to-parent support for parents who have experienced a similar loss, through correspondence, the telephone, local contacts throughout the country, meetings at the Twins Clinics and members' homes, a Newsletter, a Memorial Book and an annual Memorial Service.

Yad b'Yad (Hebrew for 'Hand in Hand') 8 Grove Avenue, London N10 2AR *Tel*: 0181–444 7134.
A Jewish child bereavement project offering seminars, courses for teachers, book list and resources pack.

6. CANCER CARE INFORMATION

BACUP (British Association of Cancer United Patients) 3 Bath Place, Rivington Street, London EC2A 3JR *Freeline*: 0800 181199 *Administration*: 0171–696 9003.

A national cancer information service offering advice and emotional support to cancer patients and their families and friends by telephone or letter. Publications on most types of cancer produced in easy-to-understand language available free of charge to individuals. A London-based one-to-one and group counselling service is available (*Tel*: 0171–696 9000) and there is a one-to-one counselling service in Glasgow (*Tel*: 0141–553 1553).

Bristol Cancer Help Centre Grove House, Cornwallis Grove, Bristol BS8 4PG *Tel*: 0117 973 0500.

Holistic treatment, courses and publications for people living with cancer.

Call Centre-Cancer Aid and Listening Line Swan Buildings, 20 Swan Street, Manchester M4 5JW *Administration*: 0161–834 6551 *24 hour Helpline*: 0161–434 8668/835 2586.

Helpline open 365 days a year run by trained volunteers all with personal experience of cancer. A support group for cancer patients, their families and carers. Offers emotional support and a 'listening ear'. Also provides information about services available to cancer patients and their families in the north-west and beyond.

Cancer and Leukaemia in Childhood Trust 12–13 King Square, Bristol BS2 8JH *Tel*: 0117 924 8844.

Helps families by funding treatment for children, by providing welfare care for the whole family and by promoting clinical research. Publications available.

Cancer Relief Macmillan Fund 15–19 Britten Street, London SW3 3TZ *Tel*: 0171–351 7811 *Fax*: 0171–376 8098.

Supports and develops services to provide skilled care for people with cancer and families. Information regarding a whole series of services available on request.

Cancerlink   17 Britannia Street, London WC1X 9JN   *Tel*: 0171–833 2451/2818   *Asian language information and support line*: 0171–713 7867 (Bengali, Hindi and English)   *MAC Helpline for young people affected by cancer*: 0800 591028. Textphone is available for deaf and hard of hearing people.
Cancerlink is the national cancer charity which supports all people through self-help, emotional support and information. Experienced staff provide free and confidential information by telephone, post and through audio and video tapes and publication.

Malcolm Sargent Cancer Fund for Children   14 Abingdon Road, London W8 6AF   *Tel*: 0171–973 4548.
Support for parents of children with cancer.

Marie Curie Cancer Care   Head Office 28 Belgrave Square, London SW1X 8QG   *Tel*: 0171–235 3325   *Fax*: 0171–823 2380.
Provides 11 Hospice Centres, a community nursing service of 6,000 Marie Curie Nurses who nurse patients in their own homes day or night; a research institute and education service for health professionals completely free of charge to the parent and family.

The National Cancer Alliance   PO Box 579, Oxford OX4 1LP
Tel: 01865 793566   *Fax*: 01865 251050.
The NCA is an alliance of patients and health professionals who are working towards improving the treatment and care of all cancer patients countrywide. To this end we speak at conferences, work with the media and with professional bodies and Trusts, and with decision makers locally and nationally. We have established a track record of patient-centred research. We provide information on cancer services including a Directory of Cancer Specialists.

Sue Ryder Foundation Headquarters   Sue Ryder Home, Cavendish, Sudbury, Suffolk CO10 8AY   *Tel*: 01787 280252   *Fax*: 01787 280548.
The Foundation's Homes provide inpatient and outpatient care for several thousand patients with a wide range of disabilities including Sue Ryder Homes specifically for the continuing care of patients with advanced cancer and Huntingdon's disease. Domiciliary care teams, respite care and bereavement counsellors also operate from some homes.

The Tenovus Cancer Information Centre College Buildings, Courtenay Road, Splott, Cardiff CF1 1SA *Tel*: 01222 497700 *Fax*: 01222 489919 *Freephone Helpline*: 0800 526527 (Monday–Friday: 9am–5pm).

Information on cancer and emotional support for patients and their families. Freephone Helpline staffed by nurses, counsellors and social workers. Drop in Centre and individual counselling. Support nurses available at Velindre and Llandough Hospitals and at Nightingale House, Wrexham.

7. HIV/AIDS CARE AND INFORMATION

ACET (AIDS Care, Education and Training) PO Box 3693, London SW15 2BQ *Tel*: 0181–780 0400 *Fax*: 0181–780 0450.
A national and international AIDS charity providing home care support throughout the UK and N. Ireland. Other offices are located in Eire, Romania, Uganda, Tanzania, Thailand and New Zealand. Also offers education and training in schools.

Body Positive 51B Philbeach Gardens, London SW5 9EB *Office*: 0171–835 1045 *Helpline*: 0171–373 9124 *Fax*: 0171–373 5237.
Among many other services provides counselling, visiting, information on dealing with death, bereavement and funerals.

The CARA Trust (Care and Resources for People Affected by HIV/ AIDS) The Basement Centre, 178 Lancaster Road, London W11 1QU *Tel*: 0171–792 8299 *Fax*: 0171–792 8004.
Offers a service of practical and spiritual support of a non-judgmental nature, bereavement counselling to those infected and affected by the HIV viral infection, training courses for carers and courses in pastoral counselling, funeral and other services, as requested.

Immunity 1st Floor, 32–38 Osnaburgh Street, London NW1 3ND *Tel*: 0171–388 6776 *Fax*: 0171–388 6371.
Advice, information and representation to anyone with, or affected by HIV or AIDS. Areas of work include employment, housing, immigration, testing, confidentiality, wills and living wills, powers of attorney. Outreach advice sessions at various centres across London. For further details or to make an appointment, please phone. No drop-in service available.

Jewish AIDS Trust HIV Education Unit, Colindale Hospital, Colindale Avenue, London NW9 5GH *Tel*: 0181 200 0369 *Fax*: 0181 905 9250.
Administration 9.30am–5pm Friday (3pm winter Fridays). Confidential Telephone Helpline: 0181 206 1696 – 7.30am to 10pm Monday to Thursday, 10am to 1pm Sunday.

Living Water Centre   38a Circus Road, London NW8 9JN   *Tel*: 0171–266 1676.
A service offering a non-judgmental welcome and support for all who are living with HIV/AIDS, their families, parents, loved ones, friends and carers. Professional counselling, spiritual direction and pastoral care are offered.

London Lighthouse   111–117 Lancaster Road, London W11 1QT
Lancaster Road and Latimer Road Sites: 0171–792 1200   *Reception*: 0171–792 2979   *Residential Unit*: 0171–229 6062   *Lancaster Road Fax*: 0171–229 1258   *Latimer Road Fax*: 0181–964 2543.
A major residential and support centre for persons affected by HIV/AIDS. Providing a comprehensive range of counselling, educational and practical services. Pastoral care, advice and support on spiritual and bereavement matters are now referred to CARA. There are several support groups, including one on bereavement.

Mildmay Mission Hospital   Hackney Road, Bethnal Green, London E2 7NA   *Tel*: 0171–739 2331   *Fax*: 0171–729 5361.
As an independent Christian charitable hospital, Mildmay provides comprehensive palliative care services for men, women and children living with/affected by AIDS. Care is given with an emphasis on quality, professionalism and respect for the rights and beliefs of each individual. Mildmay aims to remain at the forefront of research and development in this speciality by demonstrating innovative models of care and progressive educational programmes, both nationally and internationally.

National AIDS Helpline   PO Box 500, Glasgow G12 8BR   *Administration*: 0141–357 1774   *Fax*: 0141–334 0299   *Helpline*: 0800 567123.
This is a 24 hour (365 days) national phone line offering confidential advice, information and referrals on any aspect of HIV AIDS to anyone. All calls are taken by trained and paid staff. Ethnic language services available: Bengali, Punjabi, Gujerati, Urdu, Hindi, Arabic, Cantonese, Welsh (call for times).

The Naz Project (London)   Palingswick House, 241 King Street, London W6 9LP   *Tel*: 0181–741 1879   *Fax*: 0181–741 9841.
Sexual health and HIV/AIDS education prevention and support

services for the South Asian, Turkish, Arab and Irani communities. Befriending service for people with HIV/AIDS. Support groups for people affected by HIV/AIDS and for carers. Telephone Helpline Monday – Friday: 2pm–5pm in Turkish, Punjabi, Hindi, Urdu, Gujerati, Bengali and Arabic.

Patrick House 17 Rivercourt Road, London W6 9LD *Tel*: 0181–846 9117 *Fax*: 0181–741 7344.
Patrick House offers multidisciplinary team care for people whose mental health has been so affected by HIV-related brain impairment that they need 24 hour care. Every attempt is made to meet all care needs so as to avoid the need for hospitalisation. Terminal palliative care is provided when needed.

Positive Options 354 Goswell Road, Islington London EC1V 7LQ *Tel*: 0171–278 5039.
Offers a service to families with children where a family member has HIV or AIDS. Runs two schemes – a secondment scheme and a planning scheme.

Positive Partners/Positively Children Unit F7, Shakespeare Commercial Centre, 245a Coldharbour Lane, London SW9 8RR *Tel*: 0171–738 7333.
Functions wholly within the auspices of Positive partners. Hardship fund for children's needs, information network on paediatric AIDS and HIV.

The Red Admiral Project 51a Philbeach Gardens London SW5 9EB *Tel*: 0171–373 1935 *Fax*: 0171–835 1495.
Provides free counselling service for people over 16 affected by HIV/AIDS, including partners, family members, friends and carers. Counselling offered seven days a week.

The Terrence Higgins Trust (THT) 52–54 Grays Inn Road, London WC1X 8JU *Advice Centre*: 0171 831 0330 *Helpline*: 0171–242 1010 (Daily: 12noon–10pm) *Fax*: 0171–242 0121.
A telephone advice, information and counselling service for any kind of enquiry about HIV/AIDS and its social effects including advice on wills and power of attorney and the making of a living will.

8. BEREAVEMENT CARE INFORMATION

Asian Family Counselling Service   74 The Avenue, Ealing, London, W3 8LB   *Tel*: 0181–997 5749.
Provides bereavement counselling and other services in Punjabi, Hindi, Urdu and Gujarati.

The Befriending Network   11 St Bernards Road, Oxford OX2 6EH   *Tel*: 01865 316200   *Fax*: 01235 768867. Also 6 Park Village West, London NW1 4AE   *Tel*: 0171 388 9729   *Fax*: 0171 383 39508.

Bereavement Link   155 Birchfield Road, Nottingham NG5 8BP *Tel*: 0115 9263984.
An umbrella group for all bereavement services in the Nottinghamshire area. Holds conferences and study days on all aspects of bereavement.

Bereavement Trust   Stanford Hall, Loughborough, Leicestershire LE12 5QR   *Tel*: 01509 852333.
A national network and umbrella service for bereavement support services.

The Camden Bereavement Service   Kings Cross Road, London, WC1   *Tel*: 0171–833 4138.
Offers practical and emotional support to the bereaved and also contact with a trained and supervised volunteer.

Compassionate Friends   53 North Street, Bristol BS3 1EN   *Helpline*: 0117–953 9639   *Administration/Fax*: 0117 966 5202.
A nation-wide organisation of bereaved parents offering friendship and understanding to other bereaved parents after the death of a son or daughter from any cause whatsoever. Personal and group support. Quarterly newsletter, postal library and range of leaflets. Support for bereaved siblings and grandparents. Befriending rather than counselling.

Cruse Bereavement Care (National Organisation for the Widowed and their Children)   Cruse House, 126 Sheen Road, Richmond, Surrey TW9 1UR   *Administration*: 0181–940 4818   *Fax*: 0181 940

7638 *Helpline* (speaking directly to a counsellor): 0181–332 7227 (9.30am–5pm weekdays only).
A national organisation for bereaved people offering a service of counselling by trained people, a parent circle (group counselling for the widowed parent with dependent children) advice on practical problems, and opportunities for social contact.

Elizabeth Kübler-Ross Foundation   Unit 309, Panther House, 38 Mount Pleasant, London WC1H 0AP.
It organises workshops and sells books, tapes, videos. Elizabeth Kübler-Ross is happy to receive mail, but not to answer it – 33613 North 83rd St, Scottsdale, AZ 85262, USA.

Foundation for Black Bereaved Families   11 Kingston Square, Salters Hill, London SE19 1JE   National organisation offering advice, counselling and support to black bereaved families and consultancy and training to organisations. Please write for more information.

Gay Bereavement Project   Unitarian Rooms, Hoap Lane, London, NW11 8BS *Tel*: 0181–455 6844 *Helpline*: 0181–455 8894 (7pm–midnight).
Advice and support for homosexual persons on the death of their partners and help with services.

Hammersmith and Fulham Family Welfare Association Bereavement and Counselling Service   Family Welfare Association, 21 Kempson Road, London SW6 4PX   *Tel*: 0171–736 2127.
Staffed by volunteers, trained and supervised by a qualified social worker, who co-ordinates the service and allocates clients. Weekly visits according to need.

Jewish Bereavement Counselling Service   PO Box 6748, London N3 3BX   *Tel*: 0181–349 0839 (24 hour answerphone) or 0181–343 6226. Offers emotional help and support to members of the Jewish Community. Provides information concerning Jewish bereavement customs to voluntary and community organisations. Offers trained volunteer counsellors who will visit the bereaved for as long as necessary. Operates mainly in NW and SW London and the London Borough of Redbridge, but can refer enquirers to bereavement projects elsewhere in the country.

Lesbian and Gay Bereavement Project Face to face counselling service at I CARE, Islington N1. Sundays 2–6 pm. Call for an appointment. *Bereavement Helpline*: 0181 455 8894 (7 pm to midnight daily) *Office*: 0181 200 0511.

London Association of Bereavement Services (LABS) 356 Holloway Road, London N7 6PN *Tel*: 0171–700 8134.
Umbrella organisation with over 70 bereavement projects in the Greater London area. A charity whose members have all been bereaved or surviving a disaster. Their purpose is to share their common experience to provide support and guidance to those affected by disaster.

National Association of Bereavement Services 20 Norton Folgate, London E1 6DB *Administration/Fax*: 0171–247 0617 *Helpline*: 0171–247 1080.
An umbrella organisation that can suggest help for those bereaved by the whole spectrum of deaths – from natural deaths to post-disaster counselling.

The National Association of Victim Support Schemes (NAVSS)
Cranmer House, 39 Brixton Road, London SW9 6DZ *Tel*: 0171–735 9166.
Support for families of murder victims – through offering time to talk about the incident. Also support for relatives of murder victims. Local support schemes throughout the country.

National Association of Widows 54–57 Allison Street, Digbeth, Birmingham B5 5TH.
Support, friendship, information and advice group for widows. Branches throughout the country.

National Black Bereavement Foundation 25 Baysham Street, Camden, London NW1 *Tel*: 0171 388 5551.

National Gay Funeral Advice Helpline 218 Kennington Park Road, Kennington, LONDON SE11 4DA *Tel*: Freephone 0800 281 345.

Orchard Project (The) Orchard House, Fenwick Terrace, Jesmond, Newcastle-upon-Tyne NE2 2JQ *Tel*: 0191–281 5024.
Financed by Barnados, the Project provides support and counselling to

bereaved families and children in the Newcastle area. The service aims to be very flexible in recognition of the fact that every individual's circumstances and response are unique. Also runs workshops and an educational service to community and professional groups.

PACE (Protestant and Catholic Encounter) 174–184 Ormeau Road, Belfast BT7 2ED *Tel*: 01232 232864.
In association with Women Together, PACE trains people to visit families bereaved due to violence.

Portsmouth Baby Loss Support Group Rita Fraser, 14b Lovedean Lane, Portsmouth, Hants, PO8 8II *Tel*: 01705 592958.
Offers support and comfort to those who have lost a baby as a result of a miscarriage, ectopic pregnancy, stillbirth or termination for foetal abnormality.

Rigpa 330 Caledonian Road, London N1 1BB *Tel*: 0171–700 0185
Tibetan Buddhist centre founded by Sogyal Rinpoche. Runs courses on death and dying.

SAMM (Support After Murder/Manslaughter) Cranmer House, 39 Brixton Road, London SW9 6DZ *Tel*: 0171–735 3838.
National organisation offering emotional support to family and friends of someone who has been killed.

SOS Shadows of Suicide 6 Denmark Street, Bristol, Avon BS1 5DG
A group within Compassionate Friends, set up to help parents of children who have taken their own lives and to put them in touch with other parents.

Unitarian Churches Essex Hall, 6 Essex Street, London WC2R 3HY *Tel*: 0171–240 2384.
Unitarian ministers conduct flexible funerals without dogma.

War Widows Association of Great Britain 17 The Earl's Croft, Coventry CV3 5ES *Tel*: 01203 503298.
Advice for all war widows. Can supply a local contact.

9. FUNERAL/MEMORIAL SERVICES

Cremation Society of Great Britain   2nd Floor, Brecon House, 16/16a Albion Place, Maidstone, Kent ME14 5DZ   *Tel*: 01622 688292.
Can tell you the nearest crematorium to you. Publishes a free booklet on 'What You Should Know About Cremation', and a directory of crematoria.

The Federation of British Cremation Authorities   41 Salisbury Road, Carshalton, Surrey SM5 3HA   *Tel*: 0181–669 4521.
The only authority which sets codes of practice, monitors standards of operation and offers technical advice. Produces statistical information. Promotes crematorium technicians training scheme. Publishes advisory handbooks and leaflets, plus 'Resurgence', a quarterly journal.

The Memorial Advisory Bureau   139 Kensington High Street, London W8 6SX   *Tel*: 0171–937 0052   *Fax*: 0171–937 9254.
To meet the demand for the provision of facilities for commemorations after cremation and a reaction against unreasonable restrictions on memorialisation. Runs an advisory service for those planning memorial sites, and supports individuals in all matters concerning memorialisation.

Memorials by Artists   Snape Priory, Saxmundham, Suffolk IP17 1SA   *Tel*: 01728 688934.
A nation-wide service to put people in touch with designer-carvers who make individual memorials with beautiful lettering and carving. Produces booklet which contains articles, advice and photographs.

National Association of Funeral Directors   618 Warwick Road, Solihull, West Midlands B91 1AA   *Tel*: 0121 711 1343.
Its main purpose is to enhance the standard of funeral service throughout UK and be of service both to its members and to the general public. Has a training programme with a 'Diploma in Funeral Service'. It encourages all its member to adhere to the 'Code of Conduct'. Most Funeral directors belong to this association.

Natural Death Centre   20 Heber Road, London NW2 6AA   *Tel*: 0181–208 2853. *Fax*: 0181–4521 6434.
An educational charity aiming to improve the quality of dying and to act as a society for those dying at home. Publications include Living Will and booklist (for information pack send 6 first class stamps), 'The Natural Death Handbook', 'Before and After', and 'Green Burial'. Also offers workshops, seminars for nurses, information on funerals without undertakers, burial on private land, nature reserve burial grounds, cardboard coffins etc. Most of its publications are accessible free on the Internet 〈http://www.protree.com/worldtrans/naturaldeath.html〉

National Funerals College   Bredan House, High Street, Duddington, Stamford PE9 3QE   *Tel*: 01780 444269   *Fax*: 01780 444586.
The National Funerals College works to stimulate better practice for the sake of the dead and of the bereaved. It organises training and educational programmes and promotes local and national co-operation between the interested groups involved in decisions about arrangements and facilities for funerals.

National Gay Funeral Advice Helpline   218 Kennington Park Road, Kennington SE11 4DA   *Tel*: Freephone 0800 281345.

National Secular Society   47 Theobalds Road, London WC1X 8SP   *Tel*: 0171–4043126.
This organisation will advise on secular funerals.

Pagan Hospice and Funeral Trust   BM Box 3337, London, WC1 3XX.
Produces newsletter, information leaflets and does hospital visiting and support.

10. ANCILLARY ORGANISATIONS

Art Therapy – The Creative Response The Old Coal House, Station Road, Ardleigh, Colchester CO7 7RR *Tel*: 01206 230003 *Fax*: 01206 396354.
Registered Art Therapists working in palliative care, AIDS, cancer and loss. Aims to promote awareness of the appropriateness of art therapy in these areas to allied professions and the general public and to provide support for art therapists working in this field, through workshops, conferences and information pack (price £2.50).

British Association for Counselling 1 Regent Place, Rugby, Warwickshire CV21 2PJ *Tel*: 0178 857 8328 *Fax*: 0178 856 2189.
A membership organisation for counsellors and those involved in counselling which also provides a counselling and psychotherapy information service for the general pubic. An A5 stamped addressed envelope should accompany requests for information.

British Humanist Association 47 Theobald's Road, London WC1X 8SP *Tel*: 0171–430 0908.
Concerned with moral issues from a non-religious viewpoint, provides and advises on non-religious funerals.

British Holistic Medical Association Rowland Thomas House, Royal Shrewsbury Hospital, Shrewsbury SY3 8XF *Tel*: 01743 261155.
Aims to promote an awareness of holistic (whole person) approaches to health care, that balance mind, body and spirit, among practitioners and the public.

British Organ Donor Society (BODY) Balsham, Cambridge CB1 6DL. *Tel*: 01223 893636.
A voluntary organisation offering emotional and informative support to donor, recipient and waiting recipient families, intensive care units and theatre nurses. It supports various aspects of organ transplantation. It supplies and co-ordinates information requested by professionals, media, involved family and general public.

Campaign Against Drinking and Driving (CADD) 83 Jesmond Road, Newcastle-upon-Tyne NE2 1NH   Tel: 0191-281 1581.
Support and help for families of people killed by those convicted of drunken and irresponsible driving.

Centre for the Study of Complementary Medicine 51 Bedford Place, Southampton SO1 2DG   *Tel*: 01703 334752.
Aims to be involved in practice, teaching and academic research with the complementary therapies. Deals with general inquiries.

Contact Family Support 170 Tottenham Court Road, London W1P 0HA   *Tel*: 0171-383 3555.
Support for those with special needs.

The Council for Music in Hospitals 74 Queen's Road, Hersham, Surrey KT12 5LW   *Tel*: 01932 252809/252811   *Fax*: 01932 252966.
Provides live concerts given by carefully selected professional musicians in hospitals, homes and hospices throughout the UK. The hospice concerts may take place in a variety of venues, for example, the day room or chapel. If requested, music is taken to individual bedsides.

Holiday Care Service 2nd floor, Imperial Buildings, Victoria Road, Horley, Surrey RH6 7PZ   *Tel*: 01293 774535.
Advice and information on holidays, helpers and travel arrangements for disabled and disadvantaged people.

Independent Living Fund PO Box 183, Nottingham NG8 3RD *Tel*: 0115 942 8192.
Financial assistance for people receiving higher rate of Attendance Allowance to enable them to receive care at home.

Institute of Family Therapy 43 New Cavendish Street, London W1M 7PG   *Tel*: 0171 935 1651
Counsels bereaved families and those with someone in their family seriously ill. The service is free but donations are welcome to help other families.

National Association of Councils of Voluntary Service 3rd Floor, Arundel Court, 177 Arundel Street, Sheffield S1 2NU   *Tel*: 0114 278 6636.

181

Provides information about local councils for voluntary service, who in turn can supply details of local voluntary organisations.

National Council for Voluntary Organisations (NCVO) Regents Wharf, 8 All Saints Street, London N1 9RL *Tel*: 0171–7134 6161. Supplies information about national voluntary organisations. With sister bodies in Belfast, Edinburgh, Caerphilly and Welshpool. Aiming to promote, support and facilitate voluntary action and community development throughout the U.K.

National Federation of Spiritual Healers Old Manor Farm Studios, Church Street, Sunbury-on-Thames TW16 6RG *Tel*: 01932 783164. Offers advice and publishes a directory.

Pain Association, Scotland Cramond House, Kirk Cramond, Cramond Glebe Road, Edinburgh EH4 6NS *Tel*: 0131 312 7955. A national association offering personal and group support to those suffering from the effects of cancer and painful illness and to their caring relatives and the bereaved.

Pain Relief Foundation Rice Lane, Liverpool L9 1AE *Tel*: 0151 523 1486. Devoted to multidisciplinary research on the causes and the relief of chronic pain. Has information services.

Patients' Association 8 Guildford Street, London WC1N 1DT *Tel*: 0171–242 3460. Aims to advise individual patients and carers on patient's rights, complaints procedures and access to health services or appropriate private self-help groups. Promotes patients' interests nationally to government, professional bodies and the media.

Red Cross Medical Loans Service British Red Cross, 3 Grosvenor Crescent, London SW1X 7EE *Tel*: 0171–235 5454. Can supply medical equipment for short term loan.

Samaritans 10 The Grove, Slough, Berks SL1 1QP *Tel*: 01753 532713 *Fax*: 01753 819004. Always there at any hour of the day or night to offer confidential emotional support to those in crisis and in danger of taking their own lives. There are 200 centres in the UK and Eire. Look in the phone book under 'S' for your local branch or call 0345 909090.

Share-a-Care (National Register for Rare Diseases) 19 Coxwell Road, Faringdon, Oxon SN7 7EB.
Puts sufferers of rare diseases and their families in touch with others with the same condition. Send an SAE for information.

Voluntary Euthanasia Society 13 Prince of Wales Terrace, London W8 5PG *Tel*: 0171–937 7770.
Campaigns to change the law so that doctors can respond to requests to die from terminally-ill patients. Distributes the Living Will, an advance directive against unwanted medical treatment. Produces publications.

Welfare State International, The Celebratory Arts Company The Ellers, Ulverston, Cumbria LA12 1AA *Tel*: 01229 581127.
Artistic director John Fox offers consultancies for imaginative memorial services, lanterns, urns, painted coffins, etc. Publications include 'The Dead Good Funeral Guide'.

Will Information Pack Help the Aged, St James's Walk, Clerkenwell Green, London EC1R 0BE *Tel*: 0171–253 0253.
An excellent free information pack.

Wireless for the Bedridden 159A High Street, Hornchurch, Essex RM11 3YB *Tel*: 01708 621101
Provides radio and television facilities to needy housebound invalids and aged poor in the UK who cannot afford them.

Woodland Trust Autumn Park, Dysart Road, Grantham, Lincolnshire NG3 6LI *Tel*: 01476 74297.
Plant a tree scheme to remember loved ones; also commemorative groves.

(Every effort has been made to ensure that the information is correct and up-to-date. The author would welcome notices of any changes for possible future editions.)

Notes

Chapter 1: Death, the Ultimate Mystery

1. THOM, KENNEDY, *The Southwark Cathedral Service Programme*, November 1996.
2. RINPOCHE, SOGYAL, *The Tibetan Book of Living and Dying*, Rider, 1992, p. 31.
3. WALTER, TONY, *Funerals and How To Improve Them*, Hodder & Stoughton, 1990, p. 51.
4. KRAMER, KENNETH, *The Sacred Art of Dying*, Paulist Press, N.Y., 1988, p. 12.
5. Ibid., pp. 18–19.
6. Ibid., pp. 22–23.
7. GOODMAN, LISL M., *Death and the Creative Life*, Springer Pub. Co., 1981, pp. 3, 4.
8. PECK, M. SCOTT, *Further along the Road Less Travelled*, Simon & Schuster, p. 49.
9. KELSEY, MORTON, *Reaching the Journey to Fulfilment*, Harper Row, San Francisco, 1989, p. 133.
10. GIBRAN, KAHLIL, *The Prophet*, Heinemann, p. 94.

Chapter 2: Flowing into the Beyond

1. BAILEY, SIMON, *The Well Within*, Darton, Longman & Todd, 1996, p. 3.
2. RINPOCHE, SOGYAL, *The Tibetan Book of Living and Dying*, Rider, 1992, p. 259.
3. KÜBLER-ROSS, ELIZABETH, *Death, the Final Stage of Growth*, Routledge & Kegan Paul, 1986, p. 166.
4. KRAMER, KENNETH, *The Sacred Art of Dying*, op. cit., p. 188.
5. JAMES, WILLIAM, quoted in Kramer, op. cit.
6. Ibid.
7. KRAMER, op. cit., p. 193.
8. Ibid.

Chapter 3: Spirituality of the Dying

1. FEINSTEIN, DAVID and MAYO, PEG ELLIOT, *Mortal Acts*, Harper, San Francisco, 1993, pp. 84, 85.
2. WAKEFIELD, GORDON, *A Dictionary of Christian Spirituality*, SCM, 1983, p. 361.

3. FORTUNATO, JOHN. E., *Aids: The Spiritual Dilemma*, Harper Row, San Francisco, 1987, pp. 7, 8.
4. WEENOLSON, PATRICIA, *The Art of Dying*, St Martins Press, N.Y., 1996, pp. 250–51.
5. STOLL, R., 'Guidelines for Spiritual Assessment' in *American Journal of Nursing*, Sept. 1979, p. 1574.
6. DICKENSON, DONNA and JOHNSON, MALCOLM, *Death, Dying and Bereavement*, Sage Publications, 1993, p. 221.
7. WEENOLSON, op. cit., p. 109.
8. CASSIDY, SHEILA, *Light from the Dark Valley*, Darton, Longman & Todd, 1994.

Chapter 4: The Mysterious Soul

1. SHELDRAKE, RUPERT and FOX, MATTHEW, *Natural Grace*, Bloomsbury, 1996, p. 65.
2. WILSON, ANDREW (ed.), *World Scripture: A Comparative Anthology of Sacred Texts*, Paragon House, N.Y., 1995, p. 230.
3. COUSINEAU, PHIL (ed.), *Soul, an Archaeology*, Thorsons, 1995, pp. xix–xx.
4. SHELDRAKE, RUPERT, *Seven Experiments That Could Change the World*, Fourth Estate, 1994, p. 96.
5. ACHTEMEIR, PAUL J., *HarperCollins Bible Dictionary*, HarperCollins, 1996, p. 1055.
6. Ibid.
7. RICHARDSON, ALAN and BOWDEN, JOHN, *A New Dictionary of Christian Theology*, SCM Press, 1994 (new ed.), p. 548.
8. TILBY, ANGELA, *Science and the Soul*, SPCK, 1994, pp. 2, 3, 9.
9. HILLMAN, JAMES, *Re-visioning Psychology*, Harper Row (Colophon Edition), 1977, p. ix.
10. SHELDRAKE and FOX, op. cit., pp. 73–75.
11. WALSHE, M. O'C., *Meister Eckhart – Sermons and Treatises, Volume III*, Element Books, 1987, p. 131.

Chapter 5: Growing through Bereavement

1. FEINSTEIN, DAVID and MAYO, PEG ELLIOT, *Rituals for Living and Dying*, Harper Row, San Francisco, 1990, p. 172.

Chapter 6: Hope of Life Beyond

1. *The New Jerusalem Bible*, Pocket Edition, Darton, Longman & Todd, 1985.
2. RING, KENNETH, *Heading towards Omega*, William Morrow & Co., 1985, p. 35
3. HARPUR, TOM, *Life after Death*, McCellan & Stewart Inc., 1991, pp. 52–53.
4. ZALESKI, CAROL, *Otherworld Journeys*, Oxford University Press, 1985, p. 7.

5. RING, op. cit., p. 83.
6. Ibid., p. 87.
7. Ibid., p. 146.
8. HARPUR, op. cit., p. 61.
9. ZALESKI, op. cit., p. 205.
10. HARPUR, op. cit., p. 61.
11. KÜBLER-ROSS, ELIZABETH, *Death, the Final Stage of Growth*, op. cit., p. x.
12. COHN-SHERBOK, DAN and LEWIS, CHRISTOPHER, *Beyond Death*, Macmillan, 1995, p. 3.

Chapter 7: Rites of Passage: One
1. ROOSE-EVANS, JAMES, *Passages of the Soul*, Element Books, 1994, p. xiii.
2. FEINSTEIN, DAVID and MAYO, PEG ELLIOTT, *Rituals for Living and Dying*, Harper, San Francisco, 1990, p. 41.
3. ROOSE-EVANS, op. cit., p. 95.
4. Ibid., p. 40.
5. Ibid., p. 9.
6. Ibid., p. 68.
7. Ibid., p. 52.
8. FEINSTEIN and MAYO, op. cit., p. 15.
9. RINPOCHE; SOGYAL, *The Tibetan Book of Living and Dying*, op. cit., pp. 103–104.
10. Ibid., p. 245.
11. Ibid., p. 247.

Chapter 8: Rites of Passage: Two
1. GAWTHORP, DANIEL, *Affirmation*, New Star Books, Vancouver, 1994, pp. 76–7.
2. SANDYS, SEBASTIAN, *Embracing the Mystery*, SPCK, 1992, p. 60.

Chapter 9: World Religions' Approach to Dying and Death
1. KRAMER, KENNETH, *The Sacred Art of Dying*, op. cit., p. 43.
2. Ibid., p. 145.
3. Ibid., p. 125.
4. Ibid., p. 136.
5. Ibid., p. 125.
6. MOSLEY, CHARLES, *Debrett's Guide to Bereavement*, Hodder & Stoughton, 1995, p. 147.
7. KRAMER, p. 43.
8. MOSLEY, p. 109.
9. KRAMER, p. 58.
10. MOSLEY, p. 192.

Chapter 10: **The Funeral Service**

1 ELIOT, T. S., *Collected Poems 1902–1962*, 'East Coker', Faber & Faber, 1963 edition, p. 196.
2. BENTLEY, JAMES, BEST, ANDREW and HUNT, JACKIE, *Funerals, a Guide*, Hodder & Stoughton, 1994, p. 43.

Chapter 11: **Co-creating a Service**

1. ROOSE-EVANS, JAMES, *Passages of the Soul*, op. cit., p. 85.
2. BARNES, MARION, *Funerals to Celebrate*, Simon & Schuster, 1991, p. 81.
3. ROOSE-EVANS, JAMES, *Inner Journey, Outer Journey*, Rider, 1987, p. 67.
4. LEVINE, STEPHEN, *Who Dies?*, Gateway Books, 1991.

Further Reading

ALBERY, NICHOLAS, ELLIOT, GIL and ELLIOT, JOSEPH, *The Natural Death Handbook*, 1993

ALBERY, NICHOLAS and others, *Creative Endings*, Natural Death Centre, 1994

BADHAM, PAUL and BALLARD, PAUL, *Facing Death: An Interdisciplinary Approach*, University of Wales Press, 1996

BARASCH, MARC IAN, *The Healing Path: The Soul Approach to Illness*, Penguin/Arkana, 1993

BARNES, MARIAN, *Funerals to Celebrate*, Simon & Schuster, 1991

BERTMAN, SANDRA L., *Facing Death: Images, Insights and Interventions*, Hemisphere Publishing, 1991

BLAKELY, ANGELA, *When the Corn is Ripe*, Veritas, 1993

BOERSTLER, RICHARD W. and KORNFIELD, HULENS, *Life to Death*, Healing Arts Press/Deep Books, 1995

BOWKER, JOHN, *The Meanings of Death*, Cambridge University Press, 1991

BRADFIELD, J. B., *Green Burial: A Natural Death*, Centre Press, 1993

BRODKEY, HAROLD, *This Wild Darkness – The Story of My Death*, Fourth Estate, 1996

CALLAHAN, MAGGIE and KELLEY, PATRICIA, *Final Gifts, Understanding and Helping the Dying*, Hodder & Stoughton, 1992

CAPLAN, SANDI and LANG, GORDON, *Grief's Courageous Journey – A Workbook*, New Harbinger, 1995

CARSON, RICHARD and SHIELD, BENJAMIN, *Handbook of the Soul*, Piatkus, 1996

CASSIDY, SHEILA, *Light from the Dark Valley*, Darton, Longman & Todd, 1994

CLARK, DAVID and SARAH, *The Dark Uncertainty*, Darton, Longman & Todd, 1993

CLAYTON, SHELAGH, *After a Death*, Robson Books, 1996

COMUDET, HUBERT O.P., PRENDERGAST, MARTIN and SOWERBY, TESSA, *Positive Rites: Liturgical Resources for World AIDS Day*, 1996

DARLING, DAVID, *Soul Search*, Villard Books, New York, 1995

DE HENNEZEL, MARIE, *The Intimate Death: How the Dying Teach Us To Live*, Simon & Schuster, 1997

DOMINICA, SISTER FRANCES, *Just My Reflection*, Darton, Longman & Todd, 1997

DONNELLY, KATHERINE FAIR, *Recovering from Loss of a Loved One to AIDS*, St Martin's Press, New York, 1994

DOORE, GARY, *What Survives?*, TACHER, Jeremy P. Inc., California, 1990

DRIVER, TOM F., *The Magic of Ritual*, HarperSanFrancisco, 1991

EADIE, BETTY, J. *Embraced by the Light*, Aquarian Press/HarperCollins, 1992

EVANS-WENTZ, *The Tibetan Book of the Dead*, Oxford University Press, 1960

FARRELL, MICHAEL, *The Facts of Death*, Robert Hale, 1991

FEINSTEIN, DAVID and MAYO, PEG ELLIOT, *Mortal Acts: Rituals for Confronting Death*, Harper, San Francisco, 1993

FITZGERALD, HELEN, *The Mourning Handbook*, Simon & Schuster, 1995

GOLDING, CHRISTOPHER, *Bereavement*, Crowood Press, 1991

HARPER, TOM, *Would You Believe?*, McClelland & Stewart Inc., 1996

HILLMAN, JAMES, *The Soul's Code*, Random House, New York, 1996

IRONSIDE, VIRGINIA, *You'll Get over It: The Rage of Bereavement*, Hamish Hamilton, 1996

ISRAEL, MARTIN, *Life Eternal*, SPCK, 1992

JALLAND, PAT, *Death in the Victorian Family*, Oxford University Press, 1996

KEANE, COLM, *Death and Dying*, Mercier Press, Dublin, 1995

KEARNEY, MICHAEL, *Mortally Wounded*, Marino Books, Dublin, 1996

KELEMAN, STANLEY, *Living Your Dying*, Centre Press, California, 1974

KIRKPATRICK, BILL (Ed.), *Cry Love, Cry Hope*, Darton, Longman & Todd, 1994

KÜBLER-ROSS, ELIZABETH, *Death Is of Vital Importance*, Station Hill Press, 1995

KÜBLER-ROSS, ELIZABETH, *On Life after Death*, Celestial Arts, California, 1991

KUENNING, DOLORES, *Helping People through Grief*, Bethany House Publishers, 1987

LAZARUS, RICHARD, *The Case against Death*, Warner Books, 1993

LEE, CAROL, *Good Grief: Experiencing Loss*, Fourth Estate, 1994

LEVINE, STEPHEN, *Who Dies?*, Gateway Books, 1991

LIGHTER, CANDY and HATHAWAY, NANCI, *Giving Sorrow Words*, Warner Books, 1990

LITTEN, JULIAN, *The English Way of Death*, Robert Hale, 1992

LONGACRE, CHRISTINE, *Facing Death and Finding Hope*, Century, 1997

LUARD, ELIZABETH, *Family Life*, Corgi Books, 1996

LYNCH, THOMAS, *The Undertaking – Life Studies from the Dismal Trade*, Jonathan Cape, 1997

MA'SU'MIA'N, FARNA, *Life after Death: A Study of the Afterlife in World Religions*, Oneworld Publications, 1996

MALONEY, S. J., *Where Is Thy Sting?*, Alba House, New York, 1984

METRICK, SYDNEY BARBARA, *Crossing the Bridge*, Celestial Arts, 1994

MONETTE, PAUL, *Afterlife*, Abacus, 1996

MOODY, RAYMOND, *Life after Life*, Bantam, 1976 (new edition)

MOONEY, BEL, *Perspectives for Living*, John Murray, 1992

MOORE, OSCAR, *PWA – Looking AIDS in the Face*, Picador, 1996

MOORE, THOMAS, *Care of the Soul*, Piatkus, 1992

MORGAN, ERNEST, *Dealing Creatively with Death*, Zinn Communications, New York, 1994

MULLEN, GLEN H., *Death and Dying*, Penguin, 1986

NULAND, SHERWIN, B., *How We Die*, Chatto & Windus, 1994

PARKES, COLIN MURRAY, *Bereavement*, Penguin, 1983

PARKES, COLIN MURRAY; LAUNGAHI, PITTU and YOUNG, BILL, *Death and Bereavement Across Cultures*, Routledge, 1997

PECK, M. SCOTT, *In Heaven on Earth (A Vision of the Afterlife)*, Simon & Schuster, 1997

PINCUS, LILY, *Death and the Family (The Importance of Mourning)*, Faber & Faber, 1997 (new edition)

REANNEY, DARRYL, *The Death of Forever*, Souvenir Press, 1995

RIEM, ROLAND, *Stronger than Death*, Darton, Longman & Todd, 1992

ROOSE-EVANS, JAMES, *Passages of the Soul: Ritual Today*, Element Press, 1994

SARDELLO, ROBERT, *Facing the World with Soul*, Harper Perennial, 1992

SEELE, PERNESSA, *Who Will Break the Silence?*, The Balm in Gilead, New York, 1995

SHARP, JOSEPH, *Living Our Dying – Reflections on Mortality*, Rider, 1996

SHEEPSHANKS, MARY, *The Bird of My Loving (A Personal Response to Loss and Grief)*, Faber & Faber, 1997

SHERR, LORRAINE, *Death, Dying and Bereavement*, Blackwell Scientific Publications, 1989

SHELDRAKE, RUPERT and FOX, MATTHEW, *Natural Grace – Dialogues on Science and Spirituality*, Bloomsbury, 1996

SIMS, RUTH and MOSS, VERONICA, *Palliative Care for People with AIDS*, Edward Arnold, 1995

SMITH, WALTER, J., SJ, *AIDS, Living and Dying with Hope*, Paulist Press, New York, 1988

SOME, MALIDOMA PATRICE, *Ritual*, Swan/Raven & Co., Portland, Oregon, 1993

STAUDACHER, CAROL, *A Time to Grieve*, Souvenir Press, 1995

STAUDACHER, CAROL, *Beyond Grief*, New Harbinger Publications, 1987

STAUDACHER, CAROL, *Men and Grief*, New Harbinger Press, 1991

STEINER, RUDOLF, *Life beyond Death*, Rudolf Steiner Press, 1995

STROMAN, MERTON and IRENE, *The Five Cries of Grief*, HarperCollins, 1993

THOMPSON, MARK, *Gay Soul*, HarperSanFrancisco, 1994

VARDEY, LUCINDA (Ed.), *God in all the Worlds: An Anthology of Contemporary Spiritual Writing*, Chatto & Windus, 1995

WALSH, MARY PAULA, *Living after a Death*, Columbia Press, 1995

WARD, BARBARA, *Healing Grief*, Vermilion, 1993

WARD, KEITH, *Defending the Soul*, Oneworld Publications, 1992

WILCOCK, PENELOPE, *Spiritual Care of Dying and Bereaved People*, SPCK, 1996

WILSON, ANDREW (Ed.), *World Scriptures: A Comparative Anthology of Sacred Texts*, Paragon House, New York, 1995

ZALESKI, CAROL, *The Life of the World To Come*, Oxford University Press, 1996

ZUKAV, GARY, *The Seat of the Soul*, Rider, 1990

Acknowledgements

The following sources are gratefully acknowledged for their use in the anthology section of this book:

'Morning has Broken' by Eleanor Farjeon, from *The Children's Bells*, OUP; *The Road Less Travelled* by M. Scott Peck, Century Hutchinson, 1983; *Death is of Vital Importance* by Elisabeth Kübler-Ross, Station Hill Press Inc, 1995; *Man's Search for Meaning* by Viktor Frankl, reproduced by permission of Hodder and Stoughton Limited; *Markings* by Dag Hammarskjöld translated by W. H. Auden and Leif Sjoberg, Faber and Faber Ltd; *Acquainted with the Night: A year on the frontiers of death* by Allegra Taylor, HarperCollins Publishers, 1989; 'Not Easy to Accept' by Monica Furlong, from *Short Prayers for the Long Day*, HarperCollins Publishers, 1978; 'Blessing' by Simon Bailey from *Sheffield Diocesan Board Social Responsibility Service*, copyright Diocese of Sheffield; *Forms of Prayer for Jewish Worship, Volume 1 Daily and Sabbath Prayer Book*, Reform Synagogues of Great Britain, London, 1977; *Prayers of Our Hearts: In words and action* by Vienna Cobb Anderson, Copyright © 1991 by Vienna Cobb Anderson, All rights reserved, Used with permission of The Crossroad Publishing Company, New York; 'Anointing' by Jim Cotter, from *Healing – More or Less*, Cairns Publications, 1990; 'The Blessing of God' and 'O God of the Living' by Jim Cotter, from *Prayer at Night*, Cairns Publications, 4th edition 1991; Extracts from *The Book of Common Prayer*, the rights in which are vested in the Crown, are reproduced by permission of the Crown's Patentee, Cambridge University Press; 'Blessed are you, our God, . . .' and 'Loving God, we pray . . .' from *Positive Rites: Liturgical resources for World AIDS Day* edited by Martin Pendergast; No. 4 in Pastoral AIDS Series, published by Catholic AIDS Link, 1996; *The Man with Night Sweats* by Thom Gunn, Faber and Faber Ltd; 'Throughout our lives . . .' from *Love is Stronger than Death* by Peter Kreeft, © 1992 Ignatius Press, San Francisco, All rights reserved, reprinted with permission of Ignatius Press; 'I believe you died in God's will . . .' from *Kontakion for you Departed* by Alan Paton, reprinted with permission; *Gitanjali* by Rabindranath Tagore, Macmillan; *Story of My Life* by Helen Keller, reproduced by permission of Hodder and Stoughton Limited; 'The question is not how to survive . . .' and 'When I think of death . . .' from *Wouldn't Take Nothing for my Journey Now* by Maya Angelou, Virago Press; *Souls on Fire* by Elie Wiesel, Penguin, copyright © Elie Wiesel, 1972; *The Prophet* by Kahlil Gibran, the National Committee, 1951; *Grace and Grit* by Ken Wilber, © 1993, reprinted by arrangement with Shambhala Publications, Inc., 300 Massachusetts Avenue, Boston, MA 02115; Verses from 'Morning Prayers' by Dietrich Bonhoeffer, from *Letters and Papers from Prison*, enlarged edition, SCM Press,

191